Customerpocalypse™

How the next generation of customers could destroy your company and what you can do about it.

Alan Trefler
Cambridge, Massachusetts

This special limited edition of Customerpocalypse by Alan Trefler is intended for selected and in-
vited readers to provide additional conversations and observations that will find their way into the
next edition of the book. The author wants to hear from you: about what you think about Customerpocalypse, your challenges and opportunities in facing the next generation of customer, delivering a
world class customer experience, and whether technology helps or hinders.

Please post your public comments to Twitter: #Customerpocalypse or LinkedIn: Customerpocalypse
Group. You can also email your feedback to: customerpocalypse@pega.com or comment at www.
pega.com/community/pega-blog/customerpocalypse.

This book was set in Minion by Pegasystems Inc. Printed and bound in the USA.

Library of Congress Cataloging-in-Publication Data

Trefler, Alan, 1956 -

Customerpocalypse: How the next generation of customers could destroy your company and what
you can do about it.

ISBN: 978-0-615-81276-2 (softcover: paper)

Preface for Reviewers

This book is the product of decades of engagement with many of the world's most sophisticated organizations. I would like to thank the clients who have shared their views on the imminent threats, as well as their managerial and technological responses. Their journeys are the real story of this book, and it has been a privilege to see first-hand how insight and innovation can lead to differentiated success.

Capturing and refining these ideas has been a journey in itself. Let me thank the team of Brian Callahan, Scott Cooper and Russell Keziere for invaluable assistance in getting to this point.

Feedback is greatly appreciated. In particular, we welcome additional examples of firms that have rallied around the concepts in this book – or have missed-the-boat. Please send any comments to Customerpocalypse@pega.com, or to me directly at alan.trefler@pega.com.

Thanks!

Alan

Cambridge, Massachusetts

Table of Contents

Chapter 1

Why Customers Hate You

A lot of companies across the globe are going to die over the next few years, not because of macroeconomic stress but because there is an entire emerging generation of customers who hate doing business with them. These companies are going to die from some form of *customer stress*. Death may come as the result of self-inflicted wounds the company should have known to avoid, which means it's kind of like suicide. It may come from involuntary manslaughter by a new generation of customers. Or these new kinds of customers may just outright murder companies they decide should be put out of their misery.

Who are these customers? They trace their ancestry first to the Millennials, also known as Generation Y. The concept itself comes from an editorial in *Ad Age* in 1993, which attempted to describe the teenagers of that time and how they differed from Generation X, the name given to the generation born after the post-World War II baby boom popularized by the novelist Douglas Coupland.[1] When *Ad Age* coined the Gen Y term,

---

[1] Douglas Coupland, *Generation X: Tales for an Accelerated Culture*, New York: St. Martin's Press, 1991.

it applied to kids 12 and younger at the time, and was meant to refer to those kids who would become teenagers over the subsequent 10 years.

The Millennials term is widely credited to William Strauss and Neil Howe from work first published in 1991.[2] You may also have heard of them referred to as Generation We, Generation Next, and the Net Generation. They account for about 75 million people in the United States alone. The generation's earliest days are just around the time digital technologies for the general public first appeared, beginning with Apple's first personal computer, the IBM PC, and Microsoft's early PC operating system. They grew up with digital technology, and came of age as it, too, came of age, beginning its slow, steady march to ubiquity. Over the course of their lives, digital technology has become a commodity. Millennials are also the generation that grew up with play dates and adolescent team sports that awarded everyone a trophy for playing in the soccer game, whether they won or lost. This "ethic" figures into how they view the world and the relationships they have with your business as your (potential) customer.

Diane Theilfoldt and Devon Scheef aptly synopsized their characteristics in a 2004 article. Millennials are (among other things) "self-inventive/individualistic;" they "rewrite the rules;" they consider institutions irrelevant; the Internet is their world; they don't just use but "assume" technology is there for everything; and they "multitask fast." [3]

From this Millennial/Gen Y generation, another name emerged, Generation C. The name works in part because, as entertaining as Douglas Coupland's declaration of Generation X was he did us the disservice of choosing a letter far too advanced along in the alphabet to continue with his naming convention. More important is that unlike the Gen X and Gen Y names, Gen C includes a characterization within its very name.

"[T]he C stands for CONTENT, and anyone with even a tiny amount of creative talent can (and probably will) be a part of this not-so-exclusive trend."[4] These are the young people who are responsible for – and who revel in – all manner of content on the World Wide Web. They post and curate. They are the self-proclaimed editors of Wikipedia. They made YouTube the amazing repository of content that it is today.

Despite its relative youth, this group influences every aspect of our lives and wreaks havoc on many businesses.[5] Gen C accounts for about 75 million

---

[2]William Strauss and Neil Howe, *Generations: The History of America's Future, 1584 to 2069*, London: William Morrow & Co., 1991. See also Strauss and Howe, *Millennials Rising: The Next Great Generation*, New York: Vintage, 2000.

[3] Diane Theilfoldt and Devon Sheef, "Generation X and The Millennials: What You Need to Know About Mentoring the New Generations," *Law Practice Today*, November 2005, at www.americanbarorg.lpm/lpt/articles/mgt08044.html#author

[4] "Generation C: An emerging consumer trend and related new business ideas," *Trend Briefing*, February 2004, at www.trendwatching.com/trends/generationc_html

[5] See, for example, Larry Weber, *"Everywhere: Comprehensive Digital Business Strategy for the Social Media Era"* Hoboken, N.J.: Wiley, 2011.

people in the United States alone. Still growing in size by leaps and bounds, largely now from the emergence of new economies in much of the less-developed world and changing economies in places such as Russia, China, and India, Gen C is fast becoming the largest group of consumers in the entire world.

Gen C has really come into its own with the shift in the meaning of the C. I observe that today there is actually a Gen C-1 and a Gen C-2, coexisting in time. Gen C-1, which came first, are generally older than Gen C-2. They are the members of Gen C who *publish*.

With the evolution of the mobile Web, Gen C evolved from *content to communicating, computerized, clicking*, and finally, *connected*. It's the advent of *connected mobility* that has given rise to Gen C-2. This component of the larger Gen C arose with the sudden democratization of communications and the unmediated access to personalized mass communication, exemplified by Twitter, but not exclusive to that technology tool. They are the ones who use on-the-spot messaging to create flash mobs and take down repressive governments during the Arab Spring.

If Gen C-1 is the *publish* or *post* segment, Gen C-2 is the *ping* part of the group. Gen C members have gone from asynchronous communication through email and Facebook to always-on, always-linked interactions that are synchronous, happening in real time. Gen C-2 is even helping drive a move away from email.[6]

More relevant to the discussion here is that Gen C is the generation that pushed connectivity to the point where are the 10.5 billion active memberships across at least 158 online social communities—and that's exclusive of Facebook and YouTube, which add another one billion each.[7] Gen C is why every company has a Facebook page and a Twitter account, even if most corporate types using them have little idea, or in many cases absolutely no idea, what they are doing.

Great Expectations

As a whole, Gen C has some major expectations that create big challenges for companies. For instance, they expect to be able to log on to your website and perhaps even talk to someone in your call center at the same time. They expect your company to be as centered around them as they are centered on

[6] Michael B. Farrell, "E-mail gets a cold shoulder," *The Boston Globe*, March 29, 2013, at www.boston.com/business/innovation/2013/03/29/mail-gets-cold-shoulder/Fy9cD2PmWFFUAKuNiAdbN/story.html

[7] Craig Smith, "(March 2013) How Many People Use the Top Social Media, Apps & Services, Digital Market Ramblings, at http://expandedramblings.com/index.php/resource-how-many-people-use-the-top-social-media/

themselves. If they know something, they expect you to know it, too. They don't care whether you have separate divisions to handle products or services they buy from you. In fact, if you use that as an excuse for why you had to ask a stupid question (yes, in this world there are stupid questions); they will come to hate you even more.

Gen C customers have no patience when you try to sell them some lame product they would never consider in a million years. If they have a problem, they expect you to fix it in a way that makes sense.

Fail a Gen C customer, and she may or may not tell you how she feels. The best case for your company is that she just puts up with it and keeps on with what she is already doing with your business. That particular best case is not too likely. What is more likely is that she will tell all of her connected "friends" about how you failed and how she is taking her business elsewhere. The website Yelp has been a popular online destination for members of Gen C. Maybe you've seen a post like this on Yelp:

> *Tried out Super Falafel, the new place in my hood, and it hella crap. Will never go back. Surly counter help, everything lukewarm, don't take cards. Sorry to Falafel City, my old standby near work. Still great after all these years!*

The post is seen by lots of other people, and online "friends" of the "OP" (original poster) might even get notifications when one of their friends posts. They then comment and add their own experiences—with business implications that should be obvious.

Someone among the friends and followers may even revert to their "content" roots and share the experience on a website that was set up for no reason other than to mock your company and the many stories of how it has failed Gen C. These kinds of websites proliferated thanks to Gen C. Some have called them "suck sites," as in Company X "sucks," and they reflect anger based on genuine experiences.

It's Too Easy To Lose Customers

There are countless tales of companies really messing up with Gen C customers. A recent one involves Netflix, a company that had actually embraced the idea of connective collaboration with customers in the ways it did business, and drove the giant Blockbuster video store chain into oblivion. But in 2011, Netflix made a crucial mistake from which it has recovered but for which it is still apologizing. The company was hell-bent on driving its customer base to the world of online, streaming content and reconfigured its business model. But Netflix forgot that its connected customers had their own ideas about how they wanted to do business with the company and were inclined to see anything even remotely coercive as inherently evil. They weren't about to have some company—even one they had previously loved—try to change their behavior.

Netflix soldiered on, rolling out a series of tone-deaf pricing policies and new limitations on its service offerings. In doing so, Netflix came close to putting itself in the very shoes it had fitted for Blockbuster. Fortunately for the company, wisdom prevailed and the policies were reversed, largely limiting the damage to about 18 months of excruciating pain and an erosion of trust that needed rebuilding.

The Netflix debacle played out across social media platforms, blogs, and everywhere the new generation of connected customers post, chat, talk, kvetch, promote, and detract. The company fell victim to the new Gen C of customers who have expectations unlike anything businesses have ever seen and had to reverse itself.   By the way, if you think websites for complaining about companies are insignificant, take a look at netflix.pissedconsumer.com or amplicate.com/hate/facebook.

To companies like Netflix, add the electric company, cellphone providers, the cable company, and any number of businesses with which Gen C interacts, and that are responsible for people wanting to rip wires out of their walls, flush their phones down the toilet, or throw their televisions out the window. The last thing Gen C customers want any part of is knowing that you are making business decisions to influence their behavior. They'll object, they'll drop you and tell their friends. That's the end of it, and you'll probably never recapture any of those customers.

This truly is a matter of survival. Right now, to a lot of companies, figuring out how to deal with Gen C looks like a matter of evolving existing value propositions to recapture prosperity. Believe me, that won't last long. There's a big difference between prosperity and survival, and when the time comes that it's only about survival, it will simply be too late for a lot of companies.

An Ominous Future

If what you've read so far is causing some angst, you're not alone. A lot of companies feel this sense of doom, even if they can't put their fingers on precisely why and even if they don't realize how ominous it really is. For most of them, the angst is not so much about an impending death or decomposition but about having lost a sense of control. And if you've lost control, and fail to get it back quickly, your business *will* die—even if it dies through decomposition.

What does it look like for a business to decompose? It's what happens when you can't bring new offerings to market in a way that keeps your customers engaged. It's the outcome of your customer satisfaction scores trending in a downward spiral. It's your fate when you can only find people who have heard how difficult it is to do business with you. Or maybe your expense ratios are out of control, and when you try to fix them, your customers rebel—because you've taken steps that mess with them directly. Maybe you try to improve efficiency on the backs of your customers by seeking to influence their behavior in ways they just don't accept. You impose limitations they object to. Perhaps you load on more fees, which they object to—remember the fiasco of banks charging customers to talk to a teller?! What a way to drive efficiency by punishing your customers instead of encouraging them to do the things that will be more efficient, but that they will also enjoy!

Cellphone providers right and left have been cutting out unlimited data plans. This is an important element of the relationship customers have with their cellphone companies, and in making this change providers are putting a gun to the head of their customers. Do cellphone companies really think that people who once had unlimited plans aren't going to react negatively to having their data access metered? Highly unlikely!

U.S. cellphone providers failed to anticipate this problem when they first began to roll out their plans for smartphones. They didn't predict how the use of data would evolve on those smartphones. The European companies hedged, never offering a totally unlimited data usage plan. So, the Americans will be blamed for taking something away from customers, and the Europeans will not. Some say the mistake was about expense ratios, but more likely it was sloppiness in product introduction —an ungrounded anticipation of the market and the subsequent cost or retrenching. But whatever the reason, it's not a situation you ever want to put yourself in.

Have you ever met anyone who actually likes paying taxes? Yet, companies continually impose taxes on their customers. Exorbitant overdraft fees at banks. Roaming charges on your cellphone. You travel to Canada, make some calls, and the next thing you know you have an extra $300 on your bill because you didn't have the right plan.

Are You Provoking Your Customers?

Whenever businesses reflexively set things up to herd customers into certain group behaviors, they create disdain and dissatisfaction. Customers in general don't react well to these kinds of things. Gen C customers broadcast their disdain into their social worlds. They have a natural inclination against being thought of in a purely transactional way. They don't like it when you treat them like prisoners to your conception of how to do business with them.

Of course, if you're losing control of your customers because you aren't doing a very good job of meeting their expectations, there are plenty of models you can turn to for clues on what it takes to make customers very loyal. Take the Apple stores. Go by the Apple store in Boston and you'll see how easy it is for Apple to make customers happy. People are lined up outside the store before it opens, hoping to see someone at the Genius Bar, where Apple provides free-of-charge service advice and training on all of its products. Someone will come out and talk to each person waiting, suggesting that she or he make an appointment rather than wait. The appointment is booked on an iPad for, say, 20 or 30 minutes after the store opens. The employee suggests you wait somewhere more comfortable, like the nearby Starbucks. When you return at the appointed time, you're seen at the Genius Bar. On the spot. Or, if things are really busy, the employee who came outside promises to call at a certain time to let you know of available appointments. And he calls you at that precise time.

How difficult can any of that be? Not too much ... but it does take a very conscious change of mindset. Apple, rather than putting the burden on its customers, engages its customers proactively.

Still, it's not as simple as emulating Apple. Just as you are taking steps to ensure your survival from the Gen C onslaught, the whole thing is about to spin away again. It turns out there's a newer and even more ferocious threat at your doorstep, because if Gen C represents a daunting challenge to retain customers who, once lost, you may never get back, what follows in the evolutionary development of customers ought to terrify you.

Welcome to the Nightmare

Gen C customers may just hate you. The up-and coming generation of customers may choose the path of trying to kill you.

These new customers are blowing up the very notion of customer relationship management. They're not interested in a "relationship." They most certainly do not accept being "managed." And if that doesn't sound ominous enough, they don't even waste a minute hating doing business with you, like Gen C customers would. They can't hate being your customer, because they reject the very notion of being a "customer" of anyone—period. A customer, they believe, is someone businesses try to control. These up-and-comers expect to be the ones in control.

No, I am not describing Generation Z, one of the names given to people born from the early 2000s to the present day to distinguish them from Millennials or Generation Y. You may have heard some of the other names that have been given to this group, because the name that will emerge as the leader seems still to be up for grabs.[8] Other names have included the Homeland Generation, Generation@, Net Generation, and iGeneration. A noted marketing firm has proposed the Pluralist Generation, or Plurals. In my view, all these names are wrong. These people, when they talk of Generation Z (by whatever name) are really talking about Gen C-2. And in doing so, they are *missing a lot!*

Just as Gen C includes a characterization within its very name, so too does this next generation. Meet Generation D. As you learn more about them, and realize how unprepared you are for their ascendancy, you may think of that D as "doom" or "death" or "destruction." To understand how they "work," think of the D as standing for three things, depending on the moment: *Discover, devour, demonize.*

Fail a Gen D customer and you'll be lucky to get something like the Yelp post from earlier in this chapter about the restaurant. More likely, the post will be something like this sent out on Twitter:

> *never doing business again with _____ bank totally f**ked my account went to ____ bank and switched accounts great experience recommended*

The Tweet is then re-tweeted and seen by thousands. Before you can do anything about it, you've been demonized.

---

[8] Bruce Horovitz, "After Gen X, Millenials, what should next generation be?" USA Today, May 3, 2012, at usatoday30.usatoday.com/money/advertising/story/2012-05-03/naming-the-next-generation/54737518/1

"Don't Sell to Me!"

Gen D does not want to be sold to. Being sold to is being controlled. No, the seamless experience they desire with your business, to which they would probably never admit, is based on wanting to discover you and your product or service. So, on top of all that connectivity, you have to figure out how to facilitate their discovery, proactively but invisibly, to create the illusion that they are discovering all on their own. They are looking for something that makes even connectivity and connective collaboration seem old-fashioned, and they want that invisible magic. They want *radical authenticity,* and when they discover something they like, they devour it.

If you're older than Gen D (and even Gen C), you have most likely always had a relatively passive relationship with your bank, phone company, or any other business with which you deal. When you learn your bank contributed to the financial meltdown by selling your sub-prime mortgage as part of a bundle of securities in an effort to make a quick profit, you may despise it and you might even take some political action, like voting or even protesting. But while you probably don't see it as a personal betrayal by another human being, a Gen D customer may.

Gen D redefines loyalty. The totems or artifacts of loyalty have changed drastically in the run-up to Gen D's emergence. At banks, those artifacts once were passbooks for savings accounts, which have gone the way of the dinosaurs. At grocery stores, a half-a-century ago, they were S&H Green Stamps, collected over time with purchases and redeemed—as a gift for your loyalty—for things you would never just go out and buy. Green Stamps were a physical manifestation that led a customer to the sense that you didn't just make purchases at the grocery store, but also that you were rewarded with something in return. You were building value together. Today, that artifact has disappeared, replaced by the automatic discount on specific items at the store when you hand over your savings card, which also gives the store the capability to track your every purchase carefully for future and even instant marketing in the form of on-the-spot coupons.

These examples are transactional loyalty systems. Gen C might accept the word "loyalty" in that context. Gen D members want nothing to do with the idea of loyalty, as such. While most companies are grappling with connectivity and the challenge of Gen C customers, these new Gen D customers want nothing short of trust, transparency, and total openness. If they want loyalty, and expressed it as such, they'd say it's *your loyalty* to them. The authenticity they demand is visceral, and if they sense that you're trying to make them *think* you're giving them autonomy but are really trying to sneak a little M (for management) into the equation, they will have a problem and you will have a bigger problem. Meanwhile, it's hard to imagine that there isn't someone out there who is busy figuring out how to start a successful business that sells whatever product or service you sell but in a way that corresponds precisely to how these new Gen D consumers think.

Another characteristic of this generation is that their reactions vacillate between extremes. Their discovery and experience of you may cause them rapture, which means they want to devour you (in a good way), but it can just as easily cause them to demonize you. We saw the beginnings of this demonization more generally in Gen C, but the Gen C reaction is more on the passive-aggressive side. They post about you, drop you, and that's the end of it. The worst "D" you might get from this is to be summarily *dismissed*.

Gen D, though takes things to a different level, at both extremes. They experience amazing levels of affection with products and companies, even if they don't see them as products and companies. They're in love. They willingly reveal private information, like checking in on Four Square when they come to your retail location. They love Apple, for instance, in a kind of embodiment of the "I'm a Mac and you're a PC" advertisements of a few years back. You're either great and loved raptly, or you're really uncool, untrustworthy, and hence demonized.

This active demonization is a unique characteristic of Gen D. They don't create "suck sites" like those mentioned earlier, because those are meant to push people in a certain direction. Gen D is a generation of people who *pull*. While Gen C shoots their experiences out into the world and waits for you to come to them for details, Gen D puts it in your face.

What Gen D does is celebrate the fail. They are the generation most associated with the meme of the "epic fail" on social media sites. They see it as a gotcha moment to share with their friends (and friends is broadly defined to include everyone they've ever known, or who is "known" by someone they know, or who they have no relationship with other than what appears to the rest of us to be the narrowest sliver of obscure commonality.) These are young people who don't mind experiencing failure because they get to post or tweet about it. Gen C-1 creates a United Sucks page on Facebook[9] and stops at that. Gen D records "United Breaks Guitars" and posts it on YouTube, watches as it goes viral (with nearly 13 million hits as of this writing),[10] and then even publishes a book about the experience.[11] Gen D launches an all-out war without any regard for the consequences.

[9] http://www.facebook.com/pages/United-Airlines-Sucks/216811830719
[10] http://www.youtube.com/watch?v=5YGc4zOqozo
[11] Dave Carroll, *United Breaks Guitars: The Power of One Voice in the Age of Social Media*, Carlsbad, Calif.: Hays House, 2012.

The table below illustrates the broad differences between Gen C and Gen D:

GENERATION C	GENERATION D
Wikipedia	Wikileaks
Facebook (unmediated; everyone is a "friend")	Reddit (mediated; rigorous peer ranking)
Online dating	Online community organizing
Fan chat rooms	Fan fiction
Laments online bullying	Reposts and retweets a list of online bullies
Gives away privacy for consumer benefits, often unknowingly	Understand privacy implications and manipulate for their own benefits
Tweets or Facebooks occasional customer service complaints	Builds elaborate "fake-brand" or videos to voice their disatisfaction
Brand loyal	Doesn't see a brand; see themselves in brands they embrace
Watches cable channels	Streams media over the Internet

Reverse Anthropomorphism

Those "I'm a Mac and you're a PC" commercials speak to a particular way in which the rapture and devouring manifests itself with Gen D customers. When they truly love a brand, they no longer see a brand. Their identity with the brand goes way beyond brand *loyalty;* they become the brand, and the brand becomes them.

Lush, a cosmetics company based in England, is a good example of this sort of rapture and devour. The company began in 1994 with one store and today has more than 800 in more than 50 countries. Lush sells a variety of handmade products it produces on its own, from soaps to shampoos to shower gels, lotions ... and more. Everything is made naturally. Lush products are completely vegetarian, nearly completely vegan, and some 60-percent free of preservatives. Not only has the company made a big deal about not using any animal fats in its products, but Lush has also become a force in the anti-animal testing community. All Lush products are tested exclusively on human volunteers, and the company refuses to buy anything from any company even remotely involved with animal testing. Pushing corporate responsibility to a limit beyond even some of the most forward-thinking companies, Lush offers a free face mask to anyone who returns five or more used Lush containers to the store, and has a public goal to have 100 percent of all the company's packaging "easily recyclable, compostable or biodegradable."

The company also gives a lot of money to a wide variety of causes that are not strictly environmental (at least in the traditional sense). You can be sure Gen D members are well aware of this, which is part of why they love Lush. To them, it isn't a company; it's just a part of their lives. And even with all these "ethical roots," there doesn't seem to be anything preachy about how Lush works.

If you've ever gone into a Lush, you've seen some of what makes Lush rapturous to young women in Gen D. The sales clerks are Gen D. They aren't pushy. They're energetic, and it's hard to imagine they're actually working. It looks like they're just hanging out, having fun and showing friends a bunch of stuff they love. Then there's how things are displayed. One marketing expert has compared it to the way fruit sellers display their wares. Everything's out and unwrapped. You can pick it up, choose your size and particular "piece" of soap, which adds to the sense of discovery. Lush has even called itself a "cosmetics grocer."

Lush is truly close to its customers. As Mark Wolverton, president of Lush North America, explains, "We don't want a store where customers come in and browse and then take their products to the salesperson behind the till. Our staff ask questions about skin and hair type and make a big fuss over each customer, so it is fun, and they have a great experience."[12] For Gen D girls, it's like having a sleepover.

If Lush is rapture, something Gen D wants to devour, what then is an example of the demon? Well, just imagine how a Gen D member feels when he looks at something online as a potential purchase, and then little advertisements for that item or similar items keeps popping up wherever he goes on the Web, over and over. Perhaps that's happened to you. You search for a new blender, for instance, and the next thing you know you're being followed around for days and days on the Web by an annoying little blender advertisement. What could be more opposite of "invisible" or "magic"? Even if you're not a member of Gen D, you probably resent this. When we first saw Tom Cruise in the futuristic "Minority Report" in 2002 being greeted with personal offers as he walked through a glass corridor it was cool; now it seems dated, intrusive and problematic.

Lush lets the Gen D customer discover, where the demon is selling to the customer. Gen D will discover new brands and will take reverse pride if they are unadvertised, such as stealth bars known only through social media word of mouth, non-traditional kick-starter funded, crowd sourced distribution of entertainment, and consumer variations of flash mobs and meet-ups. Let's look more closely at this new pattern of discovery.

"I Want to Discover by Myself!"

Gen D is very quick to form impressions, often influenced by elements borrowed from others, and they are quick to make decisions. They are willing to act on their discoveries. The members of Gen D are immersed in streams of information. They're bombarded by activity feeds and Tweets and other sorts of things that have already been largely directed at them. Given that reality, you would think they recognize that they are not discovering on their own. But they want to believe that they and their friends are the discoverers. This turns even the most advanced notions of proactive marketing on their heads and raises all sorts of issues for search engine optimization. You have to lay out honey pots in new and interesting ways so that these consumers will come upon them and never sense they were led to them. No pushing and no overt seduction. No chasing them around the Internet, like that blender.

Thinking more about this, an old-school fishing analogy comes to mind. Traditional marketing is like drag fishing the bottom, with broad

---

[12] Quoted in Kristine Ellis, "Lush," *Retail Merchandiser*, 2011, at www.retail-merchandiser.com/index.php/reports/retail-reports/94-lush-2

nets that not only pull up every possible fish but also grab license plates or whatever else may be lurking on the bottom. You drag around and just see what comes up. The best of the more proactive marketing is like spear fishing. You get to evaluate the surroundings, pick a target, pursue and catch. But dealing with Gen D is more like fly fishing. Those who fly fish will tell you that the fish selects the fly, not the other way around – and it's the fish's decision and action that gets it hooked. You have to be willing to spend a lot of time being patient as you tie flies, and then being more patient as you stand in the river with the fish, thinking all day about what might appeal to a fish. You spend hours thinking about a fish – all without disturbing the pristine setting. You may catch nothing and go home with an empty creel. Nonetheless, the shared perception must not be that you are a still, hungry hunter, but instead you are a co-participant in a shared experience. As the fish see you leaving, they "hear" you proclaim that it was a great day, even if you caught nothing.

Gen D is like those fish. They need to hear you proclaim that engaging with them in any way, shape, or form was great ... even if it's not how you really feel. In addition, just like with the fish (where you are not supposed to be selling), your approach with Gen D has to be "catch and release." In other words, you need to earn your next strike – from scratch – with another brilliant lure.

Now that's *discovery!*

The Gen D "devour-or-demonize" characteristic changes everything about how you anticipate consumers might be led to anthropomorphize, and ultimately reverse-anthropomorphize, your business. Gen D ascribes human attributes and feelings to the businesses they choose to engage with, even if they never deal with the same person twice. The businesses that have figured this out are the ones that make sure every time a customer deals with them, each and every one of their employees is part of an engaged, and engaging, organism. It's the Lush retail store. It's the Genius Bar at the Apple store.

These companies embrace reverse-anthropomorphosis as well, ensuring that the brand has a consistent personality across channels and experiences, which enables people to associate the brand with a value system they like and support. Contrast that with the businesses that come across as schizophrenic and end up being disdained and demonized.

Gen D also creates an imperative to rethink what privacy means, because there's strong evidence they have a very different conception of privacy than most of us are used to. It has a different value to them. Gen D consumers are remarkably open to giving up their privacy. This trend began with their Gen C precursors. Just consider the sorts of things they post on Facebook.

Gen D will let you watch them browse. In return, they expect not to be sold to, they expect you not to waste their time, and they are highly sensitive to anything that appears to be you taking their privacy. The Gen D privacy line seems to be situated right at the point where they think you might be profiting from their information. (Of course, they're smart enough to know that you probably are, so you really want to steer clear of anything that makes them stop and think about it.)

All of these changes have contributed to why your business may already be decomposing. Being seen as uncool could be the trigger. A failure to retool your business to meet the expectations of Gen C may be the trigger. As if that weren't bad enough, add the halo effect Gen D has on Gen C and even people of older generations. With the stage set by Gen C for the ascendant, we are all being drawn into their online social world, with all that means for us as consumers.

Yes, Gen C and Gen D are driving companies to the brink. Some companies don't even realize it. They don't see how important it is to change how they "intrude" on people. They don't understand just how intrusive customers, existing and potential, consider those injected online advertisements. No matter the upside in terms of driving business their way, these companies may be gambling with a very significant downside that could spell the beginning of their end.

Is yours one of those companies? Demographic reality is barreling down on you like a runaway train, driven by new digital technologies. Gen D is your future, and your time is limited unless you make a dramatic change in the way you think about customers and customer engagement. This kind of change is absolutely fundamental to the continuity of your business, both because your customers demand it and your competitors are sharpening their knives. Incremental change won't do the trick, unless it's in the context of an overall conception of a radical transformation over time – and a relatively short time, at that. Incremental change absent this overall conception won't work, because the nature of the change simply does not lend itself to incremental thinking. The dramatic change that's required means you have to assume a very different intellectual vantage point, and the incremental change must be in the context of a new conception, or you'll hit the wrong target.

Let's take a look at how businesses got to this point, where they actually face destruction from the very customers they should be preparing for, beginning with the biggest elephant in the room – data.

Chapter 2

Death by Data

Data can kill your business. Cost data is particularly deadly. It's the easiest to gather and the most dangerous to apply. It becomes very easy to see what a customer is doing that costs your business money, and to calibrate how different practices might be less expensive. Consider this cautionary tale:

In the mid-1990s, First National Bank of Chicago looked at some of the information it had been gathering about its customers and decided to try influencing their behavior in a way that would cut costs. The bank wanted to drive customers to its automated "Bank-by-Phone" system, which was a money saver for First Chicago, so it imposed a $2 charge on customers who wanted to get account information from a live customer service representative.[13]

---

[13] Christy Heady, "Gimmicky Banking Charges Keep Compounding," *The Chicago Tribune*, August 13, 1993, at articles.chicagotribune.com/1993-08-13/business/9308130060_1_live-teller-first-chicago-new-fees.

It's not surprising that First Chicago is long gone. Imagine telling a Gen C customer she has to pay to speak to someone in your enterprise. Then imagine trying to do business that way with a Gen D customer! But First Chicago embraced this idea of influencing customer behavior, arguing that the bank's new policy was, in fact, good customer service because it would encourage the very behavior it believed most beneficial to the bank.

Instead, what First Chicago did was *disenfranchise* its customers.

Eventually, the charges disappeared. But the idea of charging customers fees to influence their behavior didn't go away. Some business sectors became especially aggressive, trying to charge customers a fee for everything they could think of. Think airlines: Fees for checked baggage, when first introduced, were not aimed at increasing revenue so much as they were considered a way to discourage passengers from bringing stuff on trips that make the airplanes heavier and thus increase fuel costs at a time when those costs were (and still are) skyrocketing.

Again, the aim was to change customer behavior. The culmination may well be Ireland-based no-frills Ryanair's announcement in 2010 that it would charge to use the bathroom on its flights.

"Stephen McNamara, spokesperson for the airline, told TravelMail: 'By charging for the toilets we are hoping to change passenger behavior so that they use the bathroom before or after the flight.'"[14]

Fortunately, the Ryanair plan was aborted, just like the First Chicago fee to talk to a real live person. But what hasn't disappeared are the Voice Response Units (VRUs) and Interactive Voice Response (IVRs) systems each of us has to contend with every day when we try to do business. These are more of the same, imposing a behavior change when you just want to talk to someone living and breathing. No wonder nearly everyone has a visceral hatred for these systems.

There are so many other stories of bad, bad decisions being made because of cost data. Since the advent of Frederick Winslow Taylor's "scientific management" (also known as Taylorism) back in the nineteenth century, businesses have sought to improve their economic efficiency by breaking down everything about the business into the smallest parts that could be analyzed and gathering information about how much those parts cost. Companies gather cost data about goods, processes, waste, customers ... you name it. The prevalence of cost data is buttressed by accounting systems that make it easily available to decision makers. But as the tales above show, it's a most unfortunate place to start when dealing with customers.

Clearly, the data you choose to focus on can drive you to make some really bad decisions about your customers and about influencing their behavior. Not only do Gen D customers reject being told how to behave, but they'll tell the world you're trying to manipulate them. Yet, the core of how most

---

[14] Sarah Gordon, "Ryanair confirms it WILL bring in charges for on-board toilets," *The Daily Mail* (London), at www.dailymail.co.uk/travel/article-1263905/Ryanair-toilet-charges-phased-in.html#ixzz2NS8vjKEn

companies structure their relationships with their customers continues to be based on customer data. Lots of data. Tons of data. Mega-data. Meta-data. Business people love data. They are addicted to it. It's tangible. It's reassuring.

As you accumulate more and more of it, though, you need to ask yourself this question: Is the way around the bad decisions that too often come from a data focus to use more data from which to base your decisions?

Big Data, Bigger Problem

"Big Data" is a loosely used term in information technology used to describe sets of data that are so dauntingly large, so harrowingly complex, that mere mortals can only work with them through highly sophisticated systems. Big data is difficult enough to store, let alone search through, analyze, share, and – quite frankly – make heads or tails of. But in a typical case of the tail wagging the dog, the capacity and capability of information technology on the purely technological side keeps making the problem of big data bigger and bigger. We're on our way from the terabyte to the yottabyte, which equals a septillion (that's 24 zeros) bytes.

Just in case you doubt the inexorable march to bigger and bigger data storage, consider the news in late January 2013 from a group of researchers at the European Bioinformatics Institute. They reported that they had succeeded in storing digital information in synthetic DNA molecules, and then were able to recreate the original data files without error. Sure, it was only 739 kilobytes, but "the researchers said their new technique, which includes error-correction software, was a step toward a digital archival storage medium of immense scale. Their goal is a system that will safely store the equivalent of one million CDs in a gram of DNA for 10,000 years."[15]

For businesses, big data is not a cost issue. The plummeting cost of data storage ensures that, but—as technology facilitates the aggregation of more and more data—is anyone really thinking about what data represents? Are you actually looking for and thinking more about the kinds of potential new patterns and insights that can only be detected in big data? Are you thinking about what good this might do you in a world of Gen D customers?

Autopsy of the "Customer Service Movement"

Business people have been gathering data about customers for a long time. You can see why they can fall so easily into the trap that "more of the same" will halt the impending customerpocalypse. After all, data has been at the

---

[15] John Markoff, "Double Helix Serves Double Duty," *The New York Times,* January 28, 2013, at www.nytimes.com/2013/01/29/science/using-dna-to-store-digital-information.html?_r=0

center of just about every aspect of how companies have tried to figure out how best to deal with their customers over the decades. They've gone from ad-hoc approaches to more disciplined approaches to full-blown programs centered on customer "engagement" and customer "relationships." Eventually, an entire industry emerged around what is called Customer Relationship Management (CRM). Note that nasty word "management" that Gen D abhors, which was supposed to create alignment with customers wherever they were heading and thus prevent the very demonization and destruction described in Chapter 1.

CRM is the source for a very important *false* promise about data. It concerns the infamous *360-degree view of the customer*. The 360 concept, which comes from the number of degrees in a circle, implies that if you can put your customer in the middle of a circle, you can gather up all the data about that customer from every possible angle, creating a full view of what has happened. Here's a rather typical definition of *360-degree view of the customer* that comes from an online dictionary.

A 360-degree customer view offers a total view of the customer relationship dynamic for a business.[16]

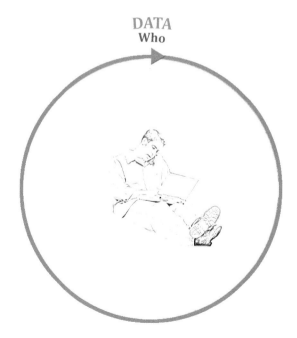

[16] "CRM Software Key Terms," at www.business.com/guides/crm-software-key-terms-34278.

Now, surrounding a customer with that customer's data can be helpful, but no customer is a standalone amoeba swimming in a round petri dish. Putting a customer in the 360 view shows you nothing about that customer's linkages. You can peer at the customer in the middle of the dish all day and all night, but you are not necessarily going to see that the customer is part of a larger "organism," a network of networks that are familial, business, and social. In other words, the 360 view alone may be interesting, but it's indubitably incomplete.

Still, the concept of the 360 customer view permeates the business world. It's everywhere. A recent Google search on *360 customer* got 428 million hits. But it has a rather checkered history, having developed out of a customer service "movement" that spawned all manner of approaches to handling customers – as in the First Chicago example, not all of them very customer-oriented. Many were driven by cost cutting.

Another trend that emerged in the customer service movement and CRM which is linked to cost data and treating customer service as a cost center, was the "industrialization" of customer service and its eventual outsourcing. Overseas call centers debuted with poorly trained, transient staff with cultural and language differences that drove customers crazy – and still do. Even customer service organizations that corrected the worst and most persistent problems typically found that staffing their call centers with the "right" people didn't help. These people still lacked the tools needed to do their jobs well.

It's important to note that the problem with data that can lead you to make bad business decisions about your customers is not just about data as information about costs. The problem runs deeper. It's about what data actually *is*.

Data is Only Memory

Here's the first thing you need to know about data. It is about the past. Data is memory and only memory. The storage facilities for data are like our human brains, packed full of memory. Now, forget about your business for a moment. Think about your life. Would you rely exclusively on your memory to make decisions in general? What about making decisions about how to deal with new people you meet?

That's what businesses do when they rely on data. And still, companies that are decomposing or are in danger of exploding continue to listen to the hardware hawkers who tell them they need to get these massive storage machines and fill them with every possible piece of data they can accumulate!

Again, ask yourself: Is more necessarily better? One thing for sure is that more data doesn't automatically translate into a better view of the customer. To be effective, 360 is supposed to accommodate all the information about a customer across time and across locale. It needs to incorporate all sorts of data, such as the history of transactions, the history of marketing interactions, the history of every sales call and service call, the history of every complaint or compliment, the results of every survey, and so on. Notice that "history" and "results" are about the past.

Even for one customer, the sheer mass of data can become very, very difficult for people to navigate, understand, and interpret quickly enough for it to do any good. How do you understand the data? Can you do a time-series analysis quickly? Does your customer service representative know how to use it all? Does she even have time to wade through it while talking to a customer?

Data becomes rapidly overwhelming, particularly when you want to deal with the whole customer. And it needs to be used all over the place, in many different venues throughout your business. There's the analytical back office, day-to-day management, the contact center, perhaps the point of contact with the customer in a bricks-and-mortar store, and so on.

Plus, data is really nothing without context. In reality, it only tells you who the customer is. Context includes, for instance, all the links that are relevant to a given customer. If your daughter calls to get a quote from your insurance company, with which you have done business for decades, she ought to be treated as part of your valued family network. If the insurer has every conceivable piece of data about you, but doesn't know that she's your daughter (her last name might be different, which is only the beginning of the challenge), the possibility that your customer service rep will mess things up increases. That list of "histories" didn't include information about family members or other business relationships that might be relevant. The traditional advocates of CRM and of accumulating more and more data have focused on quantity at the expense of distilling for these venues.

These kinds of problems have existed since the beginning of CRM. You still have to figure out how to aggregate so much data. You still have to go get it from lots of different places, which is a daunting task. It's still very difficult to train people to do the right things with whatever data you give them to work with. It's a big enough challenge just to train people to look at data and form an opinion. It's nearly impossible to train those same people to look at more and more data and understand coherently what has changed. And change it will, a lot, if you collect every available piece of data about every existing or potential customer.

To be fair, the traditional CRM and 360 advocates try to keep up with new and "better" technologies. There are hybrid combinations of data warehousing and real-time information gathering. All the attention to the technical aspects of working with more and more data comes, it seems, at the expense of the needed focus on how to use the information we already have.

Data Suicide

Let's be clear: Huge amounts of data do not translate into an automatic death sentence. You don't drown in all circumstances. It's like swimming in the ocean. There's a lot of water, but the mere fact that you dive in, or sail across it, doesn't automatically mean your death. You can swim. You can navigate. You might even get away with drinking a bit of it to slake your thirst, but since it is salt water, that's not going to last very long.

Data is far more diverse than the water of the ocean. And that's why even some accomplished data "swimmers" and "navigators" among big companies are dying or have already died from data. Sometimes, the way businesses use their customer data is the equivalent of committing suicide.

Some of the best examples are in the realm of information overload for service representatives. After all, people can only internalize and remember so much. These reps become so overwhelmed at the point of contact with customers that they end up not being able to serve customers in the manner those customers wish to be served. A failure like that is the beginning of the end for just about any business.

The banking industry provides a really good tale of suicide by data overload. Years ago, banks were desperate to become financial supermarkets. They wanted you, the customer, to engage with them around a massive collection of financial products, everything from consumer loans to investment banking.

The basic concept underlying the financial supermarket was that average customers could do everything from saving to borrowing to investing with one big company. Put retail banking, business banking, investment banking, brokerage, and in Citi's case even Traveler's Insurance, all under one roof. Banking deregulation in the 1990s made it possible, but that doesn't mean it was a good idea.

People behind financial supermarkets believed they could establish an operations side to the business that could handle every one of the diverse products for these different kinds of banking from contact centers for credit cards to mortgages. They also believed that customers would want, indeed that they would crave, these multi-line experiences with one big institution. To them, it made perfect sense. They were sure customers would respond favorably and flock to the supermarket.

But the experiment failed miserably. Why? On the one hand, customer service staff had access to enormous amounts of aggregated data about customers. They could see every transaction and every product offering. What they had was like a 360 view of the customer. More accurately, they had dozens of 360 views. Unfortunately, the technological systems they used ... well, the word is that they sucked. There was no structure to all that data, so the system offered little or no guidance to the staff people who had access to the data. They couldn't do their jobs effectively, and as they drowned in data, they took the entire notion of the supermarket down into the depths with them.

In truth, the financial supermarket idea itself wasn't wrong. What was wrong was the love and fear of data. They took a data center approach to the data and the products, forcing staff to do something at which they simply could not succeed — digest all of the customer data and gauge product suitability to that customer in real time, with no help from the technology. So, instead of achieving a 360 view, they achieved a blur.

Another type of data suicide occurs when senior management misses the big trends because they are so focused on their own narrow data. That's what happened to Sony, which ignored where its customers were heading. The company looked at its own history and the data that was all about their past, not at where things were going. The company ignored what and why customers were buying, and what that told Sony about what it should offer and how to deliver it.

Once the world leader in personal music entertainment, Sony's Walkman and Discman were outdone not only by technological changes but by how Gen C and its precursors saw their personal relationship with recorded music. Apple figured it out brilliantly, combining data about the past with what it understood about customers' future goals and objectives. In doing so, the iPod and iTunes changed the way business is done, giving new meaning to connectivity in the process. A device, music, a store, access whenever, recommendations that get smarter the more the system is used ... all seamlessly integrated. So far, this is working for Gen D, but no doubt someone much younger than you and I is figuring out the next disruptive innovation that will put Apple to the test. Perhaps *disruptive* should be added to the many meanings of the D in Gen D.

The history of business is littered with data suicides. The addiction to data underlies many stories of failure. The obsession with data feeds the false notion that a company is doing well (based on its past), while the impending changes and death threats go unnoticed or ignored. In the broadly defined entertainment industry, for example, companies miss their marks again and again, failing to see where there customers are going and ending up following the dinosaurs into oblivion.

Interestingly, the many examples of death by data seem to have little effect on how businesses operate on the whole. Rather than look beyond data, they employ increasingly complex systems that use customer data in more dynamic ways than ever before, which might have helped Sony. Still, the focus is on data. Businesses are tripping over themselves to capture every bit of customer information they can. They capture the stream of screens you went through on a website, and every item you looked at but didn't purchase, and all the selections you made to the voice-response system on the telephone, and how many seconds you spent on this or that Web page before moving on, and ... *ad infinitum*. All this with the idea that this data will inform their interaction with the customer.

Creepy Data Gathering

Casting such a wide and indiscriminate net for data can lead you to mess up in new ways you might never have considered before, and in doing so remind Gen C customers why they hate doing business with you and Gen D customers why they don't care whether you live or die. While Gen D customers are willing to share the most intimate details of their lives with their friends through social media, they become highly resentful if they think your business is gathering information about them, especially if you're going to use that to try to sell to them. They'll demonize you in a heartbeat.

The paradox is this: How do you gather the data the Gen D customer expects you to have, but wants to ignore that you are gathering it or pretend you aren't gathering it at all? And how do you do it in a way that isn't ... well ... *creepy?*

Google and other Web-based email services read your mail and mine it for keywords as a way to determine what products you might be interested in purchasing. They aren't the only businesses doing this. Your questions on automated voice-response systems are recorded and mined. So, too, are the record of your manual searches online, and every request you make to Apple's SIRI voice-controlled concierge on your iPhone.

A lot of the information that companies gather, particularly as they move to more real-time data gathering, ends up being "false positives." You send an email that mentions this or that, or make an online purchase of a baby gift for a pregnant friend. The next thing you know, you're being sold stuff only a parent would want. But you're not a parent, and this annoys you. If you're a member of Gen C, it more than annoys you. It makes you *hate* the seller and the online site that provided the information to that seller. Maybe you drop the service that got the whole thing started. Maybe you blog about it. Perhaps you even join a boycott with others who've had the same experience. If you are a member of Gen D, you set out to exact revenge. Your business might as well be dead.

If you remain unconvinced that this is a very serious problem, consider one more cautionary, true tale of Big Data.

Every time you go shopping, you share intimate details about your consumption patterns with retailers. And many of those retailers are studying those details to figure out what you like, what you need, and which coupons are most likely to make you happy. Target, for example, has figured out how to data-mine its way into your womb, to figure out whether you have a baby on the way long before you need to start buying diapers. [17]

You may have heard about this, or if not, can figure out where it's going. You may be surprised at just how serious this really is.

It turns out that Target assigns all customers "Guest ID numbers" that are linked to their names, credit cards, email addresses, and so on, and then associates those numbers with a history of every purchase and any demographic information Target is able to collect or has purchased from other sources. Over time, Target's data analysts figured out a set of products that they believed to be a strong hint that a customer was soon to have a baby (certain kinds of soaps, extra-large bags of cotton balls, and so on).

When Target sent a book of coupons for baby-related items to a teenager in the Minneapolis area, her father hit the roof and confronted a store manager. He later found out, from a talk with his daughter, that she was pregnant. Target's response to this fiasco was to change how it sends the coupons, to make it less obvious.

Now, think about everything you now know about Gen C and especially Gen D. Consider this Target story. And look at what Andrew Pole, who developed Target's pregnancy prediction model, told *The New York Times* for a story about data mining and the pregnant teen in Minneapolis.

> *How are women going to react when they figure out how much Target knows?*
>
> *"If we send someone a catalog and say, 'Congratulations on your first child!' and they've never told us they're pregnant, that's going to make some people uncomfortable," Pole told me. "We are very conservative about compliance with all privacy laws. But even if you're following the law, you can do things where people get queasy." [18]*

[17] Kashmir Hill, "How Target Figured Out A Teen Girl Was Pregnant Before Her Father Did," *Forbes*, February 16, 2012, at www.forbes.com/kashmirhill/2012/02/16/how-target-figured-out-a-teen-girl-was-pregnant-before-her-father-did/

[18] Charles Duhigg, "How Companies Learn Your Secrets," *The New York Times Sunday Magazine*, February 16, 2012, at www.nytimes.com/2012/02/19/magazine/shopping-habits.html?pagewanted=1&_r=2&hp

"Queasy," indeed! This is one of the more egregious examples of the 360 view reliance on data. In this example, there were probably multiple generations of customers – Gen C, Gen D, and even older customers— who might, *at best*, end up being very suspicious of Target. The Target story is a tale of 360 run amok.

Getting Beyond Data

In a nutshell, the big challenge going forward is to find a way to use data that makes sense, especially as the sheer amount of data accumulated becomes so large it needs a name which hasn't even been invented yet. That's the alternative to being killed by data or committing suicide. It needs to be done in a way that doesn't violate customers and potential customers, doesn't force behaviors on them that they'll reject, and creates a kind of authenticity that allows for the all-important sense of discovery we have described. You have to demonstrate to Gen D that if you're going to use their data—data they expect you to have but don't really want to know you have—you're not going to disrespect them. You have to provide them with the opportunity to discover something so awesome that their attention doesn't shift to the reality that you are tracking, mining, analyzing, and so on—in other words, so they don't spend any time thinking about the fact that you are managing someone who doesn't want to be known as your customer or be in anything that might be called a relationship with you.

But that's only part of the solution. Data alone is not going to keep you from the fate that awaits in the customerpocalypse. Data tells you about the customer's past, but what about the customer's future, especially that customer's future with your business? What good is data that tells you who your customers are if you don't know how to turn that into the right actions?

If you're viewing your Gen C and Gen D customers only through the lens of data, you're looking at the equivalent of an old, fuzzy, black-and-white TV. You're not going to see them in the colors that can reveal a deeper understanding and that can guide you to do what's best.

CHAPTER 3

Adding Judgment and Desire

Your business now has vastly more customer information than ever before. This information is no longer restricted to your internal customer database, but is complemented and frequently dwarfed by syndicated market research, sentiment and opinion inferred from voice and text analysis, and perhaps even data aggregated from social media and websites. It's that latter category of aggregated data from social media and websites that is such a game-changer, particularly when it comes to Gen D. People are no longer surprised to find that they can get richer information about your employees from LinkedIn than from your own human resources department, for example.

Sure, data can tell you *who* the customer was, but *who* is only one of the famous "six Ws" of telling a news story. You'll see shortly why you need all of six for great customer centricity just as much as you need them for top-notch journalism. Plus, data—that is, memory—can at best only *suggest* who the same customer might be tomorrow, or who might be the next customer. You need to know *why* customers are interested in engaging in general and with you in particular. You need a clear picture of *what* you should be offering to *which* customers, not just what you've already offered other customers in your massive database. You have to identify where your customers, present and future, prefer to be served—across which channels, locations, and business jurisdictions. You may have that information in your data memory, but you may not. And you need to know *how* you're going to deliver what your customers expect, not just how you've done it before.

How do you get those other Ws? How do you go from the old black-and-white TV to color? It begins with putting the data in *context*. When data alone can be confusing and even toxic, and too much data can kill you, *context* is your first line of defense.

Data in Context

Chapter 2 describes data as a brain's memory. Not only is a brain with only data mired in the past, it is largely ineffective. It cannot make decisions, and it can only replicate what has been done in the past without regard for any variables. It has no judgment. It cannot express or meet desire. When you combine memory with *intent*, data is put in context. Personality and individual interpretation are added to the mix.

Intent works bi-directionally, adding two dimensions to your view of the customer. First, *why* that customer comes to you (customer intentions) and second, *what* your own business wants to achieve with that customer (business intent). Intent expands *who* to *who/what/why*.

Customer desires and preferences—their intentions— are a rich new vein of knowledge that empowered organizations are learning to take seriously. While Gen D does not want to be sold to or "acquired" as one of your customers, they may well be willing to have a conversation with you. If you can get them to discover you so that you can listen and learn from their intentions, you will be in a much stronger position to connect and anticipate their preferences and continue the conversation. All information and no intention means the people in your business and the systems that support them become overwhelmed with too much wrong information delivered at the inappropriate time and, more often than not, to the wrong place.

In short, *intent* comprises the personality of your customers, their goals, desires, needs, and preferences. It is also your interpretations of your customer, your business objectives, and how you want to engage with those customers. If data is memory, intent is *desire* moderated by *judgment*.

Only when you combine judgment and desire with memory can you begin to transcend the fuzzy black-and-white 360 data view. Intent transforms the black-and-white data to something rich in color. You go from "just the facts" to the color wheel. Intent makes data come alive, focused and relevant. It transforms memory from simply knowledge of the past into part of a powerful knowledge tool for the present and future. It does this by transforming the reactive into the proactive. Think of data like Mount Rushmore, waiting to be worked by sculptors Gutzon and Lincoln Borglum. The sculpture of Washington, Jefferson, Roosevelt, and Lincoln they ultimately released from that massive rock was already there in the side of the mountain. Their intent released it.

From Black and White to Color

A baseball analogy to star New York Yankees pitcher C.C. Sabathia helps describe this important concept of adding color and shows how much is lacking when you rely on data alone.[19] It also illustrates how little value you get from relying on averages, as is typical with data.

Sabathia throws his fastball about 40 percent of the time as his first pitch, followed by his slider (about 25 percent), his sinker, and then, rarely, his change-up. So, a batter just coming to the plate to face Sabathia is probably preparing for the fastball. What that batter is not doing is preparing for the average of all the pitches Sabathia is capable of throwing, because in this game you cannot prepare for an average. The average is as useful to that batter as knowing that three is the average number of legs of all the barnyard animals on a farm with an equal number of cows and chickens. What practical benefit does it do you to know that kind of average? None.

How, then, does a batter make his judgment? Yes, he'll expect the fastball as the first pitch. But a major league hitter also looks at the pitcher's hands for a clue. He tries to hone in on the seams of the ball as it leaves the pitcher's hands. Those are clues that begin to add a little bit of color to the data point *fastball*. Based on what the batter sees in those clues, he uses his judgment to makes adjustments.

DATA
Who

INTENT
Why / What

---

[19] Thanks to my colleague Dr. Rob Walker for this analogy

As my colleague Dr. Rob Walker, who came up with this analogy, says, "Before you know it, you'll have a massive color palette to choose from," and a far better understanding of the customer's intent.

Adding Judgment to the Mix

With judgment added to the mix, data can be used to figure things out in a considerably more powerful way than looking at data alone. For instance, if you're a credit card company and one of your customers has two identical charges on his statement, the data alone really tells you nothing. But judgment allows you to determine that they may be duplicates, and your intent to have the best relationship with that customer may compel you to dismiss one of the charges (using some rules, of course) before he even receives the statement for review.

Here's another example, one that may resonate directly with your own experience. Let's say you call your credit card company because you received your statement and there was what you think is a discrepancy. "I don't recognize this $70 charge for "DBA/Scintilla Business Services"," you tell the customer service rep. "What are you going to do about it?"

Lots of descriptions on credit card statements are cryptic, so this problem is common. If you had aggregated not only data of charges from Scintilla Business Services, but also information about other customers who have called about such charges, you could have your system use judgment. Was the charge removed for other customers? Was it removed only to have it reapplied by the merchant and then accepted by other customers? The data can show that, and your judgment can inform intent: What are you going to do when the issue comes up again. Perhaps you have information indicating that while it's an unfortunate name for a florist to use when running credit cards, nearly every customer who calls realizes during the conversation that he had sent flowers to his wife or girlfriend. Your system could aggregate the data, apply judgment, and over time learn something that allows you to fulfill the customer's intention to have this dealt with easily and clearly, all while meeting your business intent of having a seamless interaction with the customer that results in not having to undo a legitimate charge.

All that adds *what* and *why* to the customer *who* provided by the data you keep in your business memory.

Another example is Farmers Insurance. Today, Farmers is well known for its strength as an insurer of commercial properties. The company flexes its muscle and shows this strength in its recent "University of Farmers" advertising campaign. It is a relatively new strength, though. Only a few years back, the executive leadership began to take a hard look

© Farmers Insurance Group

at its business processes and spurred a transformation that took Farmers from a market follower to a market leader.

The company saw an opportunity in an underserved market for business owners' insurance, recognizing that insurance companies typically sell businesses on rather generic policies rather than policies that are unique to the specific needs of different types of businesses. Sure, Farmers could structure unique policies of that sort, but it meant that agents had to do a lot of back and forth both with systems and back-office underwriters to get the information they needed. It could take what seemed like forever, and potential customers would too often just end up with another carrier.

Perhaps you've opened a Brazilian barbecue restaurant, a churrascaria. Congratulations. You've got all your permits, you've hired staff, and you've installed your open-pit grill to roast the endless skewers of meat your customers will soon enjoy. You know meat, but you don't know how your open-flame grill will affect the expanded fire damage coverage on your first-ever commercial insurance policy, or whether your state allows for liquor liability coverage. (Not all states do.) So, you call your Farmers agent, with whom you also have personal insurance.

It used to be that when you placed that call, your Farmers agent didn't have that information at his fingertips. Farmers agents knew houses and automobiles, but the complex thicket of rules associated with commercial insurance was too much, too complex for quick offers and results.

So, you would have to wait for days and sometimes weeks for your agent to get back to you with a quote. It would take more and more time to underwrite and check the policy, and as the underwriters dug deeper into the specifics, you might have to start over. All that back and forth added to anxiety and delay. Instead of getting ready for your grand opening, you were dealing with your insurance company, because some of the things that are common in the underwriting of a Brazilian restaurant are far from the typical questions asked on the typical business insurance application. For instance, do you have an open flame? (Or, if you're opening a pizza joint, do you plan to send drivers out in cars to deliver to customers?)

Farmers knew there had to be a better way. The company worked back from the customer experience and set as their goal a seamless experience for small commercial insurance agents and their customers. Farmers took customer intentions (give me a reliable quote quickly) and put all the data, those nasty business rules, and state and local regulations into context. Farmers has its own dedicated agents, but it also wanted to make sure that the general agents who can influence a customer to go with a particular insurance company would see the benefit of leading with Farmers.

Going beyond the data to get to intent doesn't have to be rocket science—it is about finding ways to incorporate the common sense of your most effective staff into the moments of truth with customers. Farmers Insurance made a very simple change to how it does business. It put itself in the shoes of its own agents and its customers and married data with intent. The company eliminated complexity. Farmers trained the system to remember to ask the right questions at the right time to make it easier to build a relationship with the business owner and get quotes quickly.

By organizing all the complex rules used to manage different types of risk, Farmers "wrapped and renewed" an unfriendly transaction system and transformed it into a customer-centric platform that captured intent. The transformation enabled thousands of agents, without training, to deliver tailored policies for each kind of business. Intent made the difference. By combining what Farmers wanted and what customers wanted, Farmers went from near the bottom to near the top in small commercial lines, doubling market share and achieving a 70 percent increase in umbrella policy sales.

Oh, and by the way, the new approach slashed the typical two-week wait time for a quote to about fifteen minutes.

I've seen businesses use intent, coupled with data, to increase their customers' connection. The turning point comes when they stop being slaves to data and to the impossible dream of knowing everything.

Bringing Smart to Big

Before we get to more examples of how leading organizations have married intent to data and information, it is important that you understand how we fell into data envy and what we need to do to get past it. While this might seem contrarian at a time when Big Data is touted as a panacea for what seems like everything from the common cold to the debt crisis, it's just not the case. Here's why.

When you rely on data alone, the only way to get "smarter" is to get more and more data, over and over. You have to be collecting data continually. And that data has to be cleaned and tested. A better way is to let go of the need to collect data for data's sake and instead get the right data, tested in a much more pragmatic and adaptive way than is typical. The scientific method points the way.

The scientific method has been around at least since the seventeenth century. But because marketers and other business people tend to come from a different educational and training sphere than scientists and engineers, it's only recently that they've discovered the value of rigorous testing of hypotheses. This development has also been set back by the perspective that all you need is more data and the truth will come forth.

What is the scientific method? According to *The Oxford English Dictionary,* it is "a method of procedure ... consisting in systematic observation, measurement, and experiment, and the formulation, testing and modification of hypotheses." The scientific method has five steps. The first is *observation*, followed by *hypothesis, prediction, experimentation,* and *conclusion*. It's the approach scientists take to let reality speak for itself.

That may seem difficult, but it's not. As the great English thinker Bertrand Russell once wrote, "Scientific method, although in its more refined forms it may seem complicated, is in essence remarkably simple. It consists in observing such facts as will enable the observer to discover general laws governing facts of the kind in question."[20]

Wouldn't you like to uncover facts about your customers that really matter?

The Power of Hypothesis

For our purposes, the key step in testing data and capturing intent is the *hypothesis*. Exhaustive analysis of data is too difficult, and it compels the 360-degree people to focus on perfection, which in turn leads them into the trap of gathering more and more data. It is much better to look at just enough data to form a hypothesis and then *test the hypothesis*. In other words, applying the scientific method. Getting the data to reveal some sort of "divine truth" is possible only at the end of the world, when you can look back in hindsight. But getting the data to help you uncover a

[20] Bertrand Russell, *The Scientific Outlook*, New York: W.W. Norton & Co., 1931.

customer's intentions is not only possible, but—as it turns out—relatively easy. It's as much about changing your mindset as about anything else.

The counterargument to those who insist that Big Data promises the next great improvement in customer centricity is, again, that data—no matter how much you gather—simply cannot tell you what you need to know to transcend the 360 customer view. Data will not take your business to a higher level. Big Data just for the sake of Big Data is still just more data unwedded to intent.

More than that, the over-focus on *data* causes people to skip the hypothesis step, because it can be seductive to think that the data itself can deterministically drive to a particular conclusion. But in even modestly sophisticated settings, you cannot afford to do that. You still need to take the step of using the patterns you see as a basis to create hypotheses—and then for those hypotheses to be sufficiently independent of the original data so you can really form the right judgments.

This change in mindset doesn't come naturally to most people, as another example illustrates. In one company, there was a software team that was trying to improve the performance of some key parts of the firm's information systems for a long time. But this team of a dozen or so bright, well-trained, talented software engineers kept missing its goal. So, the engineering manager and the CEO spent some time with the team to figure out why.

What was happening? The team had a singular focus to gather data to indicate where the performance gaps were coming from. But the problem—as is often the case in complicated settings—was that the results were inconsistent. Certain things would sometimes be really fast and then there would be periodic agonizing delays. The team looked at the data over and over to see whether it was "good" or "bad." They made changes to the system and then watched how the data in the system changed. They did all of this, however, without first creating a testable hypothesis.

When the engineering manager and CEO talked with the team, no one said anything like, "Well, to improve performance, I think we need to understand how the length of time of these queries becomes non-linearly worse when there are more than a certain threshold of users"—suggesting interference between these two seemingly disparate functions. A working hypothesis like that could have been tested, and, whatever the conclusion, it would have provided insight into the root causes of the system behaviors.

The absence of a hypothesis only compounded their confusion, because each change was just a shot in the dark absent a testable check on whether the data was actually making sense. Each shot in the dark did nothing to contribute to the team's understanding of what was going on.

They were just making changes, again and again, hoping that something would stick. Their work was the equivalent of randomly walking around in the hope of reaching an intended destination.

What they needed wasn't more or better data. They needed to set out on a specific path, an *intentional* path, and see whether it got them to where they needed to be.

Once the philosophy changed to create testable context that was validated to add to understanding, the issues were quickly tamed. As the old Arabic proverb goes, "Experiment adds to knowledge; credulity leads to error." Believing you see "patterns in the data" without finding ways to validate is the difference between understanding correlation (these things go together) and understanding causality (when this happens, it is caused by a certain context married with my intent to achieve certain goals).

Hypotheses teach. If you're not testing, you end up just accepting what you think the data is telling you. Using intent as a means to develop and then test hypotheses allows you to project and anticipate future behavior. This creates knowledge that goes well beyond the 360 of the 360 customer view and can be extrapolated to (and tested on) other populations.

This chapter began by drawing the distinction between a brain that has only memory and one that combines memory with desire and judgment . Unfortunately, businesses settle for just the memory every single day. It's the basic model of customer service, even of the vaunted 360 customer view. Businesses keep track of all their activities with customers, but they fail to figure out what that information *really* means about what the customer wants and intends.

As the example above of the software team illustrates, it's tough to get information systems people to solve this problem without a mindset change. Business folks end up resigning themselves to something along these lines: "Just dump out *all* the data, and I'll train my people to understand what we've got." The result is to doom the customer service people, who will drown in the overwhelming deluge of non-contextual information.

Next-Best-Action

How, then, do you work pragmatically with people in the context of numbing amounts of data, bringing judgment and responsiveness to the points of contact? An excellent example of how to apply the scientific method to integrate intent with the biggest data you can find is *next-best-action*, which allows you to bring intent into the mix with customers at just the right time, in the right context, and without overwhelming whomever is engaging with your customer. It is a win-win for you and the customer.

Next-best-action works on the premise of offering and promoting the right thing to the right person at the right time. It balances what your customer wants and needs and what your customer's interests might be with your own business objectives, and then continuously reevaluates and rebalances to optimize the outcomes. It comes close to the fly fishing analogy mentioned earlier. The next-best-action is carefully and thoughtfully constructed based on contextual information and insight.

This approach flips on its head the old-fashioned approach of creating a proposition for a product or service and then going out to find interest. By its very nature, the next-best-action approach provides the opportunity to be customer centric. Next-best-action is based on having the computer working along with the person or system, interacting with the customer across the range of applicable products—using predictive analytics algorithms to continuously optimize, prompting the customer service rep to offer what really makes sense, or communicating with the customer directly in a manner similar to a self-service environment.

A customer service representative for one of the country's leading cable television providers tells a humorous story about just how "awesome" (his word) it can be when you marry data and intent to figure out the next-best-action, what a customer really ought to be offered, and then deliver it at the perfect moment in the interaction. One day, he took a call from a "nice old lady" who wanted to get cable television in her home. As he spoke to her, the top recommendation popped up on the screen: Offer her Cinemax.

Now, Cinemax is somewhat notorious for its late-night programming block that features adult titles that have earned Cinemax the nickname "Skinemax," even in the mainstream media. The network itself even acknowledged the nickname when it used a play on the term to name its 2011 documentary series "Skin to the Max."

"She reminds me of Grandma; she doesn't want 'Skinemax,'" the agent thought to himself. So he went through the call without making the recommendation.

Then, just as he was wrapping up, the woman said, "You know, there's this show on Cinemax that my friend was telling me about. Do you guys have Cinemax?"

Good for her—but the key to success is to make that same offer to those not bold enough to have asked for it themselves. In this case, the system was right and had suggested the exact right offer. I'll bet that service rep doesn't ignore system recommendations from now on. The next-best-action, which can only be determined when data and intent have been combined and the information system is presenting what's been figured out in real time, is an approach that builds and strengthens your connections with customers. It goes well beyond the typical sales and buying experience to reshape the entire experience between customer and provider.

Adaptive Learning

Next-best-action gives you a very good idea of what to do next with your customer. But it is only useful in that moment. To give it real long-term value, you need to combine it with adaptive learning. Together, these two tools form a virtuous circle that propels you beyond 360, because you're adding a second 360-degree view of intent. The result is a much broader, sharper perspective on the customer.

Adaptive learning is how you validate that the predictive analysis that led you to the next-best-action is still optimal. It employs advanced analytics to examine the trends and patterns across millions of customers to sense what customers would prefer, what choices would satisfy their needs, and how best to anticipate and predict customer behavior. The sheer volume of data allows for inferring customer intentions. By constantly testing new and different hypotheses, this approach can reveal patterns and probabilities that work with new Big Data and all the impure, not-quite-perfect data we already have.

Can a computer predict human behavior authoritatively 100 percent of the time? Of course not. But for customers whose behavior falls within certain parameters and patterns, I've seen the success ratio for using customer data and customer intentions to craft an upgrade offer or service recommendation climb to greater than 50 percent. More than half the time the customer says yes to the predictive suggestion framed as an offer.

For instance, let's say you have three products to suggest to a customer. Let's call them Product A, which customers buy 80 percent of the time when offered based on overall sales data; Product B, which customers buy 60 percent of the time when offered; and Product C, which customers buy 40 percent of the time offered. Typically, you'd suggest Product A first, since it's most likely to result in a sale. You'd offer Product B second, and Product C third. Simply reversing that order might yield some very interesting information that would help your organization strengthen its sales. But let's look at a more specific challenge.

What do you do if you suddenly find that Product A is now being accepted only 70 percent of the time, but Product C is now also being accepted 70 percent of the time? Would you simply keep Product A as the first offer and move Product C to be second? Reversing the order might tell you something useful. And going even further, to try and learn whether there's some correlation between what customers who were now favoring Product C had bought in the past could provide even more useful information. All of that data, coupled with intent, can help your organization learn and adapt.

Organizing Your Insights

Bringing organized insight to the data teaches what to champion and what to challenge, so that you get real insights into fulfilling customer desires. Just as you're limited in how much you can learn from a single transaction, relying on data alone for learning is tremendously limiting. But add the data from transactions together, then subject that data to what you know about intent, and you not only find patterns but also get to test and refine those patterns. It's certainly not uncommon for customer behavior to change, and for what's popular and desired to change. If you want to be ahead of the curve and ahead of the trend, adaptive learning is the way to go. The more your business knows, the easier it is to match your intent with your customers' intentions and use judgment to fulfill those desires in a way that mutually satisfies.

A great example of combining next-best-action and adaptive learning can be found in some of the divisions of the wireless provider Vodafone. With more than 400 million customers and 86,000 employees in 30 countries across five continents, Vodafone supports more than 14,000 stores around the world. The company's aggressive global growth comes at a time when the entire communications industry has felt its foundations shaken by new technologies such as voice-over-Internet and data-hungry smart phones as well as new opportunities that include mobile payments and streaming media.

A fact of life for today's communications service providers is the ease with which customers can switch providers and the simple fact that it is a much greater challenge (and cost) to win a new customer than retain an existing customer. There may be no better motivation for taking customer empowerment seriously and using every means possible to improve listening.

The connection between Vodafone and its customers' intentions is as strong as any I've seen. Every time a Vodafone pay-as-you-go customer reloads her phone, she receives a next-best-action "daily special"—a new, individualized offer to make her plan better that is based on her actual usage and what Vodafone has figured out will best serve the provider, the customer, and retaining that customer. The equation works like this: Take the objectives and intentions of the customer (the *who* and the *why*), add Vodafone's own aims and what the company wishes to and can accomplish (the *what*) given the customer's own intentions, and come up with an individually tailored deal that meets everyone's objectives. Then, to put icing on the cake, provision the deal immediately upon the customer saying yes.

Customers greet these offers with considerable enthusiasm. The acceptance rate for these offers is better than half. In other words, more than half the time when Vodafone customers reload their phones, they choose to take advantage of an offer from the provider.

All this done on such a regular basis may seem like a lot of work and tweaking for Vodafone and a lot of bother for customers, but it's actually what makes Vodafone the choice of hundreds of millions of mobile phone users. The entire basis of this rests on a merger of customer intentions and Vodafone's business intent, which Vodafone has figured out thanks to the company's deep understanding that its customers expect their objectives to be *known* by those with whom they do business.

For Gen D customers, the key to achieving such a high acceptance rate with offers will be for it not to feel like pursuit, but the customer's own discovery.

In the Vodafone model, everyone benefits. The customer gets something that makes more sense for her, and Vodafone keeps her happy—and connected—without doing anything that doesn't also meet with the company's business objectives. The technology is only a tool. The important lesson here is that Vodafone, as part of its customer retention strategy, chose to invest in listening first, learning what customers really want, and then proactively tailoring the company's response to match customer intentions.

Of course, Vodafone built customer processes to operationalize its marrying of memory with judgment and desire, of data and intent. As the company well knows, it's not enough just to have the right ideas about customer centricity; you have to be able to operationalize those ideas and execute on them.

One of the best things about how Vodafone fulfills desire is that the company doesn't need to have perfect data. It may seem counterintuitive, but getting away from perfection actually unleashes the capability to go beyond the restrictive 360 view. Those wedded to the old data-centric, 360 customer view spend inordinate time and energy working on and worrying about data perfection. This is unnecessary and actually hinders customer centricity. The corollary to data perfection is data completeness. If you are driven to perfection, you feel the need to capture every single piece of data lest you miss something that might be crucial. So, businesses are compelled to gather more and more and more, seemingly without end.

In an intent-led engagement with your customer, you need to let the rhythm of the interaction guide the offer. Things about the interaction it-self— not just the analytics— have to figure into the equation. It's not just data, but "chemistry." Intent is judgment. The next-best-action may be a next question.

So, here's something worth asking yourself: How *little* data might you need to drive a successful, intent-led engagement with your customers?

Feedback Loops

Adaptive learning becomes even more powerful and valuable when you incorporate feedback loops from the interaction with customers. This creates an opportunity for your intent to become "smarter" as the inter-actions evolve.

Information technology makes it possible for a system to infer things from the interaction, in real time. For instance, a customer who is filling out an online survey may suddenly slow down. It might be because of a distraction, but it might also be the result of a lack of decisiveness. The system can use that data, shift judgment, and possibly create an offer for the customer that takes into account those areas of indecisiveness.

In other words, the interaction itself provides situational data to the overall view of your customer. By seeing the dynamic of how the custom-er is responding and not responding. you gain insights into the customer that you may have never before considered. That enhanced insight cre-ates better alignment between your business and your customers' own intentions.

Intent Goes Both Ways

To keep aligned, the best exercise is to test your hypotheses against the reciprocity principle. We have long been told that having a 360-degree view of your customer data was the Holy Grail, but what we are now learning is that if you are to leverage intent to maximize your customer centricity, you also need to *give your customers a consistent view and ex-perience of your business.* Intent goes both ways. Here's an example.

Consider a customer who has a significant small business relation-ship with his bank. He does a lot of business with the bank and there are a lot of transactions involving his business. The business uses many different services and technology solutions that the bank provides. This small business is a highly valued customer.

This same guy also maintains a personal checking account at the bank, one in which he doesn't usually keep a balance that comes anywhere close to the amount in his business account, which is in the tens of thousands of dollars.

One Monday night, when his balance in that personal account was $339.26, he wrote a check to his son for $350. The next morning, he went to the bank and deposited into his personal account a $200 check he had received in Monday's mail at home. That brought his balance to $539.26, but since the check he deposited was drawn on a different bank there was an overnight hold on making the funds available.

Tuesday afternoon, his son goes to the bank to cash the check Dad had given him. As a courtesy, the bank cashed it, despite that the funds weren't available. But the system automatically spit out a charge for being overdrawn, and on Wednesday Dad receives a notice that he his personal account had been assessed $25 for the paid check.

Now ask yourself a question. This guy is a valued customer. His business account is important to the bank. Does it make sense for the bank to charge this outstanding small business customer a $25 overdraft fee on his personal account? Of course not. It makes no sense at all.

What that bank needed is what Verizon Wireless has begun to do with its customer service representatives. They are given a discretionary "budget for satisfaction" that corresponds to each customer but which scales up to a maximum for those with a potential higher lifetime customer value. Verizon allows its representatives to use their best judgment, letting them decide what makes sense – and go a little further if they think there's a need - but conversely not always exhausting the maximum if they do not feel it is warranted. Using system-driven next-best-action intelligence together with their own human judgment gives them better capability to achieve a true optimization of the overall interaction.

Verizon's ability to use a budget for satisfaction requires organization. Now think about how the bank is probably set up, channel-wise, and how the bank's systems probably work. The monthly fee for the personal checking account is probably generated automatically. The bank employees responsible for personal checking accounts are probably not the same people responsible for small business accounts. Do they talk to each other? Do their systems prompt them to think about the two accounts and how to handle them even if they are nominally responsible for only one? The systems surely have the data that tells them the customer has these two different accounts, but do the systems capture the business intent of the bank? Again, the sensible conclusion is that *he should not be charged that monthly maintenance fee.*

The bank needs to have that intent built into its decision framework, elevating the decision above a particular bubble of product-specific rules and data. If the bank hasn't figured out not to charge the customer, the customer has probably complained. If he hasn't complained, the only explanation that makes sense is that he's not paying attention. A Gen C customer wouldn't let that slip. A Gen D customer would have set out to destroy the bank.

How do you get intent linked to data and translate that into situational thinking? Just as you have a data repository, you need to build a repository of what your business wants to do and what it has to do it with, powered by information technology. Then you empower the business people to think situationally by making it possible for them to put that technology to work directly, and in real time, to meet their needs. Companies have turned around the way they deal with customers by exciting their business people as they capture customer intentions and business intent directly. It gives the business side enabling technologies that makes their job of keeping customers connected and satisfied much easier. It builds on the concepts of next-best-action and adaptive learning to provide customer service reps with answers to questions they might not have even thought of.

Remember the "financial supermarkets" discussed in Chapter 2? That business model failed because the banks were so busy gathering data and believing that all they needed to do was offer their customers the complete range of possible services to build a strong connection. But the banks failed to address how to make sure what they were doing captured their own business intent and exactly what their customers really wanted.

OCBC Bank has taken a different approach, one that has gotten the balance right by addressing customer intentions. When you enter a branch of OCBC Bank in Singapore to open an account, you are immediately given priority and paired with a highly professional customer service specialist, who takes you to a private but comfortable and traditional working area. When the bank first rolled out its new approach, there were even professional greeters at the doors to escort new customers to these specialists.

In this special enclave, you sit side-by-side with the specialist and share a touch-screen computer with a swivel base mounted on the desk. The specialist asks about your financial planning and banking needs. As you chat, bank products pop up on the screen. Based on your profile and intent, only relevant and logical choices are offered because intent has focused the data. You make some selections and are given advice, information, and guidance regarding what additional options are available. Only *after* you are comfortable with your selections does the system ask you for identification. Normal inside-out practice would ask for the identification first, but doing so after the customer is pleased with the service selections makes a big difference. The ID is scanned on a desktop scanner and all the blanks in the forms are automatically filled in. The customer service specialist validates the information with you and then the product selections on the screen become even more aligned with your needs. The system—now that it "knows" you—is thinking about what might be best. And what it thinks is completely, totally based on data and hypotheses about that data that have been tested in context.

Vodafone and OCBC are great examples of how powerful it can be to marry data and intent. Now let's extend our C.C. Sabathia baseball analogy to this topic. Imagine you were able to marry data and intent in your head, with some kind of tiny software implant. You're facing C.C. Sabathia, and as you stand in the batter's box, the program is going through all the options, looking at all the colors, and whispering in your ear what the next pitch is likely to be. Your next-best-action will be better, and you'll see your batting average improve.

Perhaps baseball's not your game, and you're a chess player. There's an analogy to chess that makes this point about combining human judgment with the power of computer analytics very well. Garry Kasparov is a former World Chess Champion whom many consider to be the greatest chess player of all time. In an essay reviewing a book about artificial intelligence, he told numerous tales of playing against computers.[21] In his own matches with technology, he was a consistent winner, even in his first effort against IBM's much touted behemoth computer Deep Blue. His narrow victory against Deep Blue the first time turned to a loss in the rematch.

In 2005, Playchess.com—an online site—hosted a "freestyle" chess tournament. It was open to anyone, and teams could use computers. The prize money was considerable, and "several groups of grandmasters working with several computers at the same time entered the competition." Kasparov writes, "The surprise came at the conclusion of the event. The winner was revealed to be not a grandmaster with a state-of-the-art PC but a pair of amateur American chess players using three computers at the same time. Their skill at manipulating and 'coaching' their computers to look very deeply into positions effectively counteracted the superior chess understanding of their grandmaster opponents and the greater computational power of other participants. Weak human + machine + better process was superior to a strong computer alone and, more remarkably, superior to a strong human + machine + inferior process."

The same equations work in business with your customers. Writing about chess in the *International Herald Tribune*, Hartosh Singh Bal ended up making the case for next-best-action and adaptive learning in a much broader context. "So far, experiments with advanced chess suggest that

[21] Garry Kasparov, "The Chess Master and the Computer," *The New York Review of Books*, February 11, 2010.

the powers of man and machine combined don't just make for a stronger game than a man's alone; they also seem to make for a stronger game than a machine's alone. Allowing chess players the assistance of the best computer chess engine available during top tournaments would ensure that the contests really do showcase the very best chess being played on earth."[22]

How, in a business sense, do you capture the potential of that kind of tiny software implant when facing Sabathia on the mound, or the tremendous combined power of analytics and human judgment that wins chess matches? There's more to it than just data and intent. They are only two of three siblings.

In a customer relationship setting, unless the insight of next-best-action can be delivered to the right person having the conversation with your customer, it will forever remain an insight not actuated. What is happening behind the scenes of a seamless account opening at OCBC are activities that address all the accounting and regulatory requirements, funding the accounts, enabling PIN access, and issuing cards. In other words, there is *process* at work. It's a wholly new *customer-centric process* and bringing it to life is something that all the data in the world could never do.

[22] Hartosh Singh Bal, "Chessmate," *International Herald Tribune*, June 5, 2012.

CHAPTER 4

Getting It Done with Customer Processes

We now have memory (data) together with judgment and desire (intent). Combined, they create wisdom that memory alone cannot provide. But something more is needed. To be responsive, to be able to respond with that wisdom, you need some muscle. Only with muscle can you put memory and intent to work and deliver results.

In the human body, skeletal muscles—also aptly known as "voluntary" muscles—have tendons that anchor them to bone and that are for locomotion. Processes, functioning as muscle, also have an anchor or foundation, found in the remaining three of the "six Ws" discussed in Chapters 2 and 3. Data is *who*. Intent expands the list to include *what* and *why*. Like tendons in muscles, working with the brain, processes work with data and intent to complete the list, adding *when* and *where* and *how*.

Every human body depends on muscle. So, too, does your company. You certainly have processes by which you operationalize your company activities. To prepare for Gen D and the customerpocalypse, though, you need extra strong muscles. Your existing processes aren't going to stand up to the onslaught. They don't even work the right way, because they haven't been strengthened by being imbued with the orientation of your customers. You need *customer processes*.

Customer processes are what allow you to look in from your customer's perspective at your business to see it as a whole—across channels, silos, and whatever else breaks up your company into parts that potentially present a disconnected, disjointed view to the customer. Seeing the whole is a prerequisite to giving customers a seamless, coherent experience of doing business with you.

This outside-in, but also side-to-side, way of thinking about the processes that help you run your business maps a customer's intention with customer information to drive and guide a customer engagement to a completion that corresponds to what your customer wants. Gen C expects nothing less; they want what they want, and they want to know you work to give them what they want. Gen D's expectations are even greater, yet ever more subtle. They want what they want, and you had better give it to them seamlessly, without a clue that they are being sold to or managed. Otherwise, they've "gotcha." And they'll make sure the world knows about it.

The Best Action for Every Customer Interaction

To achieve seamless customer interactions you must have customer processes that make customers experience your business in a way that is personalized, and that the customer senses is unique to his or her individual situation. No process can make that possible if it isn't a customer process that fuses data and intent.

This is where the customer process needs to be especially intelligent and work particularly fast. A customer process worthy of the name needs to be able to change to meet the particulars of any given customer, on any given day, with a unique payload of specific and even one-time requests.

As we discussed in Chapter 3, Farmers Insurance and Vodafone leveraged insight into their own procedures and customers within new customer-oriented processes that put those insights to work. Farmers is a good example of reversing the inside-out thinking that characterizes traditional business processes—one process for sales and another for underwriting, for example—and embracing the outside-in model. Vodafone uses the rich breadth and depth of information to analyze probability and infer customer intentions, and then creates a brand-new customer process that wins loyalty in an intensely competitive marketplace.

In those examples, customers are already "in the door" and engaged to a greater or lesser degree. What about initial interactions with customers?

First Impressions

Everyone knows the old adage that you never get a second chance to make a first impression. These are words businesses ought to live by. To illustrate their importance, let's again use a bank as an example.

Today's banks are burdened by their past. Take a look at the old-fashioned ways so many banks inflict on their customers just to open an account. Manual forms and multiple identity checks create delays and inconvenience. For a Gen C depositor, such a combination is a deadly combination, and by the time Gen D members become a big percentage of bank customers, it will be too late for those who haven't adapted. Gen D may hardly ever step foot in a brick-and-mortar bank. No wonder customer-focused account opening is becoming a litmus test for whether a bank will be able to compete.

BB&T chose to face this challenge head on. The bank, founded in 1872, is one of the top 15 in the United States. It has a big footprint in the country, with 1,800 banking centers in twelve states and more than 30,000 employees. Like most other banks, BB&T had long employed the traditional approach to welcoming a new customer, one that had evolved over decades. A person had to come into the bank and fill out a lot of forms, and then those forms would be sent to people in the back office. Customers would wait while signature cards were filed, identities were verified, and funds were finally put into the new account. After 9/11 and enactment of the Patriot Act, things were made even more cumbersome. One section of the Act requires a more stringent "Customer Identification Program" with a larger number of documents to check.

For banks that do things this way, like BB&T used to do, new-fangled channels for signing up new customers, such as the Internet or over the telephone, don't make things any faster or easier. These channels all rely on the same old steps. At some point, the same humans in the back office are engaged and the same paper forms are required. If anything, the introduction of new channels only complicates the situation. The traditional processes saw to it that BB&T simply could not capitalize on the potential of any of the newer channels to optimize the customer experience, generate new revenue, and lower the costs that come with having people sitting in branch offices waiting for new accounts to walk in the door.

Still, as BB&T watched its competition introduce online account opening, the bank needed to do something to keep even. So, BB&T's information technology people worked feverishly to create an online account opening facility comparable to the competitors, as quickly as possible. They ended up slapping something onto the bank's website that was, of course, the same old process, but with a Web face. The results were not what the bank's executives expected—more often than not, the online applications were abandoned.

The lesson here is that simply adding a new channel doesn't fix underlying problems. The fact that the legacy processes were difficult and unfriendly was only part of what BB&T was confronting. While the Web solution allowed customers to do the digital equivalent of filling out all the forms needed to open an account, BB&T found that the bank couldn't meet the commitment it spelled out to online customers that their accounts would actually be opened in a timely manner and with no additional effort. Plus, if a customer abandoned the online account application midway through filling it out but then wanted to talk to someone on the phone or go into a branch, that customer had to start all over. There was no sharing whatsoever of anything a customer did across these multiple channels.

There's another important lesson here: Don't bake too much into a given data venue. Intent has a certain logic. You want to reach into a channel or venue where the data needs to be accessible, but you don't want to lock yourself into a channel by making that data, in a sense, part of the channel's unique system's code.

The BB&T situation was bad enough for customers in general. For Gen C customers, it spelled doom. BB&T had to fix things fast. Soon enough, Gen D will be needing banks, too. For the fix, the bank set out to do things differently. BB&T designed a new account opening process that not only automated all of the back office procedures whenever possible, but also unified these procedures with their customer-facing front-office processes. These included the processes associated with walking into a branch and dealing with a customer service representative, such as requesting a line of credit or applying for a loan. By unifying the front-office requests for service with the fulfillment of those requests in the back office, BB&T eliminated delay and errors and improved the experience for all involved.

BB&T figured out how to bring the right decision to the right place, and succeeded in providing a consistent and streamlined experience— not just a process, but a customer process. It no longer matters whether the customer goes to the BB&T website to open an account, phones into a call center, or walks into a branch. Each channel works the same way. And staff at call centers can now "pick up" so-called "abandoned applications" from a self-service channel. In other words, if you are on the BB&T website and begin to apply for a new account but then stop before completion, you can phone the bank later and talk to someone who can restart the process right where you left off.

Seamless Customer Processes

Gen C customers expect just this kind of seamlessness. Gen D customers don't expect it, but that's only because they're not really conscious of seamlessness unless you fail to give it to them. The bottom line is that Gen D cannot really conceive of things being any other way.

Using business rules to carry intent into the process, BB&T automated key functions such as ID verification, credit scoring, and credit decisions to approve, reject, or refer the application for further review. Additional areas of automation included real-time ACH funding, monitoring of funding via paper check, back-end system updates, and confirmation emails.

The results have been extremely positive. Application abandonment has decreased by half. Operational costs associated with support staff are down 75 percent, because those staff aren't needed. Time to open a new account, which in some cases had taken up to two weeks, is now just minutes. Some 90 percent of customers reported being "very satisfied" or "satisfied" with their account-opening experience with BB&T. BB&T customers no longer have to wonder why the bank has the kinds of problems that they would never, ever consider to be valid ones to have in the first place.

The solution turned into a significant amount of new business revenue as well. One of BB&T's executive vice presidents likens it to what the bank would have brought in if it had 75 or so additional, mature brick-and-mortar branches. Just opening that many new branches would have cost upwards of $500 million, but BB&T realized the value at a fraction of the cost.

For BB&T, helping their customers navigate this new channel was an opportunity to bring their customers into sharper view. The bank had invested in a 360 customer data view, but the initial experience trying to go online had demonstrated that, at minimum, BB&T needed better interaction between its staff, systems, content, and business rules. That pointed to needing another 360—*intent*. If it could automate some functions, BB&T believed it would achieve greater efficiency that would benefit customers. But beyond this, BB&T realized that its siloed information was hindering true customer engagement.

Only when BB&T addressed these problems and developed the new approach did the bank succeed. Success came from imagining its processes from the customer perspective and modeling service according to what customer processes would look like. BB&T added process muscle to its memory and its judgment. Adding yet another 360 was the key to bringing BB&T customers into a relationship driven by data, intent, and process.

From a customer perspective, channels are simple choices, and customers expect the freedom to move seamlessly from one channel to the next. Why not? They can start watching a movie on the television, pause, and then resume watching on a tablet or laptop computer. They can stream their music libraries from personal cloud storage at Amazon or Apple to their mobile phones and home entertainment systems. Why can't they have the same seamless experience with their banks?

To be fair, accomplishing seamlessness of that sort in a business setting like BB&T is far more difficult. Changing the channel changes the experience, and there are a lot of internal things the bank must address.

You need to be able to leverage the 85 percent or so of the customer experience that should be cross-channel, and make that work across channels, while also being able to perfect the venue-specific part of the experience that makes the relationship stick. But in the end, none of that matters to the customer. Customers don't really care that you have to have that capability. They don't want to know you're living up to their expectations, and how. They only want those expectations met. Period.

Getting Beyond Business Process Modeling

How do you do that in the context of process? What's the starting point for creating genuine customer processes?

Just as businesses focus on data for the sake of data, just as they miss intent time and again, businesses also tend to impose broken, inside-out processes on their customers. Even the best of these, the ones that make customer experiences better than their competitors, are more about the business than the customer. Few businesses rethink their processes completely from the customer perspective. Such is the classic problem of business process modeling, which tends to document the existing series of *internal* steps in a business line or function or channel. And what happens when there's a new channel? More often than not, those same internal steps are simply replicated.

How do you avoid that traditional business process modeling trap? To put your customer into sharper view, you need to begin thinking about processes, and continue to think about them, with one question in the forefront: How does my customer want to engage with me? Start there, and you will never make the mistake of not assuming that your customers will naturally want to be able to move from a social media interaction (e.g., a rant or rave on Twitter) to an online chat, to a call center engagement, to a visit to a physical retail location.

This is not to say that new channels are not important. Right now, mobile and social channels are the big news. Indeed, they are powerful and disruptive. They can't be constructed as isolated silos, somehow exempt from everything else and doing things their own way. Your perspective needs to be that they are just another way customers deal with your company, because that's how customers see them. And they have to be invisible as channels, because that's how Gen D will (not) see them. Once you're there, you can begin to design customer processes that put data and intent to work together.

Crossing Lines

For Prudential Group Insurance, part of one of the world's largest financial services institutions with operations in the United States, Asia, Europe, and Latin America, multiple lines of business spelled problems for customer service. The company didn't know how to handle things if a client crossed those lines. So, Prudential set out to fix things by designing the customer process from the perspective of a client specifically needing to cross lines of business as a matter of course.

Just how difficult did the old way make things for Prudential clients when they contacted their insurance provider with a new request? The company itself said that multiple silos of information translated into "an inconsistent service experience" for clients. Data was housed in eight separate silos. Staff who dealt with customers were in multiple call centers, and it was impossible to get a comprehensive view of a client. More important, it was impossible for the client to get a comprehensive view of Prudential. It took eight different systems just to service one customer, and Prudential had long needed to staff at excessively high levels just to achieve an "adequate" level of customer service. A lot of customer service representatives were sitting around much of the time.

The company set out to fix this problem by building new customer processes that mapped information and data to customer intentions and drove customer service according to those specific intentions. What they wanted was a consistent service process that worked the same way no matter how a customer tried to reach Prudential. What they created was a customer process that allowed *any* customer service associate to deal with *any* call for any product. That's precisely what customers increasingly expect—an experience in which whatever the person on the other end of the phone might be using triggers the right questions, gathers the right answers, and integrates everything together.

Similarly, American Express has put its customers in sharper view with a customer service revolution within its World Service organization. The company had long positioned the American Express brand around the actual card and the benefits that come with being an American Express member. But with the move to more and more online transactions, the company found use of the physical card was under threat. Given that reality, how could American Express retain a customer base that had been built around having that piece of plastic in your wallet, expand to capture Gen C customers and grow to engage Gen D? After all, Gen D will reach a station in life where it might make sense to discover American Express, and when that happens every Gen D member will have brought along all the characteristics that make them so uniquely desirable, and dangerous, for any business to engage.

American Express realized that the true benefit membership provides to its customers is not in the card itself, but a relationship galvanized by trust and a high level of service and attention backing up the card. So, the company decided to deepen relationships with customers by empowering customer care professionals to deliver even more outstanding service. This meant creating an integrated global network of 16,000 customer care professionals across nearly two dozen servicing locations, all focused on a relationship-driven approach to customer service.

This approach relies on active listening and creating an emotional connection with customers. American Express uses customer feedback as its primary measure of success—specifically, how likely are American Express members to refer or recommend the company to their friends and contacts. This intense focus on customer relationships has provided American Express with a loyal following of brand ambassadors that has helped the company earn six consecutive JD Power & Associates awards for highest customer satisfaction among U.S. card companies, as well as numerous other international customer service awards.

How did American Express get there? The company realized it could create better value for the company by providing greater value for its members, and that getting service right would provide a true competitive advantage. Research shows that consumers willingly spend considerably more with companies that provide great service. Surveys also show that vast numbers of consumers have stopped transactions due to subpar service. American Express knew that if it could create a more intimate relationship with its customers, it would provide greater opportunities for the company.

American Express thought about its billions of customer interactions and how they could be dealt with in a different, better way. How could the company combine data, intent, and process to differentiate itself? American Express wanted to use these elements not only to meet, but *exceed* the expectations of its members.

Customer expectations are informed by broadening service experiences across industries through multiple touch points, something American Express already knew, and that more informed consumers now share their experiences via social media. Consumers are in a very strong position of influence because of the viral nature of social media and the 24/7 access to information that mobile computing enables. The connections members make in their personal lives and via social media create opportunity for American Express.

All of this meant that American Express needed to embrace a new service paradigm and, in fact, change at American Express was driven through the service organization and managed upward. The company asked itself how it could make a positive impact in the lives of American Express members. If American Express was in the business of serving its customers, then that meant the company could no longer view interactions with customers as transactions that required reducing average handling times in order to get clients off the phone quickly. Because every customer interaction was unique, American Express needed to empower its customer care professionals to deliver on the promise of personalized care to its members. This was the only way American Express could overcome the preconceived notions members had regarding their customer service and deliver an experience that exceeded customer expectations.

This involved a philosophical shift from transaction servicing to what came to be known as Relationship Care® which recognizes that the company is in the relationship business and needs to deliver a human connection. Knowing that great brands are built upon emotion, the core mission at American Express was refocused on being the most respected service brand in the world with Relationship Care® enabling, engaging, and empowering its customer care professionals to deliver on that promise.

BB&T, Prudential, and American Express all accepted the challenge of creating customer processes. They married data and intent and put them both to work in service of an outside-in customer process rather than an inside-out business process. This is the most difficult task and has nothing to do with technology and everything to do with mindset. Old habits die hard. It is human nature to want to project your view onto the other.

Getting to the point where you can actually deliver the best possible customer process is easier said than done. You need to look past the immediate engagement or transaction and imagine that your customer will be with you for a long time, even a lifetime. How will that journey change over time? How will your customer want to interact and engage with you at different points in that relationship journey? You will need to tailor your customer processes so they are adaptable to any situation that might arise.

Building for Change

Even if you do embrace the idea of overturning your inside-out processes and replacing the way you do business with outside-in *customer processes*, you still have work to do. Just like muscles atrophy, so too customer processes can deteriorate. And just because you've figured out how to combine the 360 of data, the 360 of intent, and the 360 of process, the "muscle memory" it brings you and which serves top-tier athletes so well, is not going to serve you very long. In fact, it won't give you any sort of advantage the very next time a customer engages with you in a way that doesn't correspond to something you've already experienced. It could be the very next day after rolling out your new customer process.

Muscle memory is what allows you to replicate everyday activities that become automatic. But more than that, it is what makes those automatic actions improve with practice. Think of riding a bicycle or touch typing on a keyboard. For top-tier athletes, muscle memory is what separates your ability to serve reasonably well in a friendly tennis game and their ability to put a serve right on the line, time after time.

Patterns are part of that memory, and knowing those patterns definitely is powerful. But with your customers, muscle memory is detrimental if it is so based on patterns that your customer process—better than a traditional business process though it may be—ends up getting stuck in a repetitive, unadaptive framework.

To avoid such a situation, a customer process must be more than seamless. It must be built to be dynamic, able to shift how it works according to any particular customer situation or circumstance. How else can a customer process map to precise intentions?

In addition, your customers must experience a persistent connection. Customer processes cannot have disconnections or interruptions, and they must give the customer a consistent, unified view of your business. Making channels irrelevant to how the customer experiences your business is just as important as you having a single view of the customer.

Finally, a process that is not fluid and cannot evolve, is a process that does not simply become antiquated, but becomes a prison. Your business will change over time, perhaps over short periods. Your customers are evolving continually, perhaps even continuously if taken as a whole. The process must follow along with this evolution. Just as muscle memory needs to be retrained so the athlete can adapt to new situations, so too must customer processes be continuously recalibrated to ensure that they are working optimally.

Only when you have customer processes that actuate a seamless, dynamic, "sticky,"[23] and evolvable way of doing business with your customer can you actually put data and intent to work in order to anticipate what customers will need, prefer, or want. The insights that come from next-best-action and knowing intent are useless unless they can actually change work priorities, assign specific tasks to individuals based on the situation, automatically launch new workflows based on context, and automate anything that gets in its way. If anything, a customer process is identifiable by the sense of opportunity that is at its core.

---

[23] In Web slang, a "sticky" website is one to which people return again and again.

There are four principles of customer process to keep in mind:

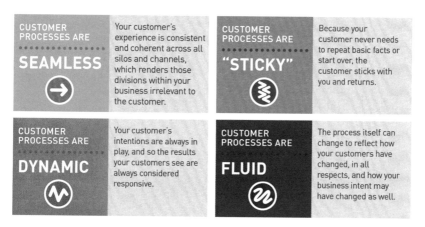

CUSTOMER PROCESSES ARE **SEAMLESS**	Your customer's experience is consistent and coherent across all silos and channels, which renders those divisions within your business irrelevant to the customer.	CUSTOMER PROCESSES ARE **"STICKY"**	Because your customer never needs to repeat basic facts or start over, the customer sticks with you and returns.
CUSTOMER PROCESSES ARE **DYNAMIC**	Your customer's intentions are always in play, and so the results your customers see are always considered responsive.	CUSTOMER PROCESSES ARE **FLUID**	The process itself can change to reflect how your customers have changed, in all respects, and how your business intent may have changed as well.

This is how you transcend the limited customer view that is all about data, add the added dimension of intent, and actuate the two to provide the kind of reciprocal customer engagement that Gen C has demanded and Gen D will assume. This level of engagement is more vibrant precisely because you allow your newest customers to get exactly what they want out of a relationship with you—to participate, inform, and converse with you, while not being sold to so much. This is the path to enabling Gen D's discovery.

A High-Definition Panorama

In a high-definition panorama, you move from black-and-white to color, and the increased detail, broader context, and greater amount of information brings new respect and new opportunities to earn customer trust.

Putting the customer into the kind of high-definition you need to face the customerpocalypse is serious business. The challenge of achieving it could well be the tipping point for larger transformational changes in your organization, but the increased customer loyalty you will attain is more than sufficient reward. An even greater incentive is that if you fail to act, you run the risk of a steadily eroding customer base that puts your business on life support (at best).

Put together the 360 data view, the 360 intent view and the 360 of customer process, and you've hit 1080, which is high-definition. Sure, the specific 1080 resolution may soon be surpassed, but the principle of high-definition will always remain. If you've seen a hockey game on television and been able to follow the puck in a way you never were able to before high-def, you understand the principle. If you know how vain Hollywood stars are and how much they hate high-def because the camera shows their age and imperfections in ways makeup seems unable to hide, you understand the principle. Apply that understanding to your relationship with your customers, and the old 360 data customer view with which this discussion began, no matter how much data you may have, pales in comparison (pun intended).

But to make this all work, you're going to have to stop paying lip service to "transforming technology" and fundamentally change how your entire enterprise thinks about, manages, and acquires technology. The stakes are too high, kicking the technology can down the road is no longer an option, not now with the looming presence of Gen D around the corner.

CHAPTER 5

Change How You Think About Technology

Why is technology at the center of how you need to respond to the challenges described in the previous chapters? The answer is simple. You have no chance of succeeding without information technology. It has already become a fundamental part of business, and for businesses that deal with diverse customer bases, have multiple products or services to sell, and do business in more than one location, the idea of going forward without technology is nothing short of ridiculous. Technology—and how it is used—is increasingly seen as the basis for differentiation and success in business.

Accenture plc, a Fortune Global 500 company and one of the world's largest consulting firms, gets it right in its Technology Vision 2013: "Without information and technology, a business is blind in today's digital world. ... Every business is now a digital business."[24]

---

[24] "Accenture Technology Vision 2013," at www.accenture.com/us-en/technology/technology-labs/Pages/insight-technology-vision-2013.aspx

The Accenture Vision continues: "The world has already changed around us, and IT is driving much of the transformation. IT is a minimum standard for how we effectively run our enterprise, but it's gone further than that. IT has become a driving force, in many situations the driving force, for how we effectively grow our companies. Every industry is now software driven; as such, every company must adopt IT as one of its core competencies. By this we mean that software is absolutely integral to how we currently run our businesses as well as how we reimagine our businesses as the world continues to change—how we redesign and produce things, how we create and manage new commercial transactions, how we begin to collaborate at unprecedented levels internally and with customers and suppliers. In the new world, our digital efforts will be the key to how we innovate and expand our business."

The Technology Vision is pointing to a Gen D world, particularly with respect to "collaborate ... with customers ..."

Finally, notes Accenture, "There is a higher order of thinking—a digital mindset—that will, we believe, separate tomorrow's most able organizations from their lesser rivals."

One sign of the expanded, refined centrality of IT in business is that in many enterprises, the marketing function is eclipsing the information technology function as the main driver of technology spending, a trend that Forbes magazine reports "shows no sign or stopping—or even slowing down—any time soon."[25]

This is strong evidence that businesses have truly become digital businesses. For the longest time, information technology—which in the business world first served to automate accounting functions—mainly served internal operations. Now, IT has become fundamental to the outward-looking parts of the business, the customer-facing parts.

To accomplish a "customer-centric approach," the Forbes article continues, "marketing needs systems in place for data collection, automated analysis and targeted distribution ..." Marketing campaigns themselves are becoming "more and more centered on customer insight and real-time analytics."

Sound familiar?

Using digital technology is the single-most distinctive characteristic of the Gen D customers for whom you need to prepare. They use it to a degree that eclipses every generation that has come before them in business history, including Gen C.

As digitalization moves into the front office and the realm of your customers, it becomes absolutely critical that you make it succeed. The

---

[25] Lisa Arthur, "Five Years From Now, CMOs Will Spend More on IT Than CIOs Do," *Forbes*, CMO Network, February 8, 2012, at www.forbes.com/sites/lisaarthur/2012/02/08/five-years-from-now-cmos-will-spend-more-on-it-than-cios-do/

digital "channel" is now as fundamental as manufacturing once was. Manufacturing, once a key differentiator, became commoditized. The digital capabilities of a business are now a key differentiator. In fact, it is emerging as a core competency, central to how a business and its employees work, but also critical to achieving competitive advantage.

How critical? The correct "digital mindset"—to use Accenture's phrase—is the difference between living and dying. Without information technology, there is no way you can break down the obstacles to the customer experience the ascendant Gen D demands. *No alternative exists*.

Your path to high-def, to the 1080 customer view that marries data, intent, and customer process into a powerful way to stay alive and thrive in the face of the coming Gen D, begins with changing how you think about technology. Everyone in your organization needs to change their mindset, so that business people and the information technology people alike, as well as the most senior executives, understand that technology should be first and foremost a way to optimize the customer experience and intelligently automate operations. Business people need to understand that technology is what will ultimately get them where they need to go or cause them to fail, and they need to be able to believe that technology can be made available to them so they can genuinely serve their customers. The IT people need to relinquish a lot of control over decisions that were once thought to be the exclusive purview of the technologists. These are the starting preconditions to avoiding failure.

The Business-IT Collision

Unfortunately, there's a lot to overcome before you can get there. Business people are frustrated. They are hugely dissatisfied with information technology at their workplaces, because it doesn't do what they want. They wonder why their experiences at home, with great devices that easily do nearly anything they want, can't be replicated at work. Why, they ask, has there been such an epic fail when it comes to achieving parity between the home and the office? They don't necessarily understand how dissimilar business systems are from their home devices, but even if they did, they probably would still insist on replication. After all, this is the twenty-first century! Going back even further, business people want to know what happened to the promise of genuine business-oriented programming.

These factors are a large part of why the relationship between business people and IT people in many companies is not one that helps the organization bring its customers into higher definition. There are too many issues of power and control and distrust, and the history of the two sides seeming to work at cross-purposes is too long.

Business people don't necessarily know what they need to know about the IT side and what it takes to build a new system, but often think they do. At the same time, IT people are too often wedded to their archaic ways of doing things, expressed in the form of a traditional development process that has largely gone unchanged over the past four decades. On top of that, IT faces enormous pressures on their budgets and views business demands as more than can be afforded.

A host of other issues get in the way of IT's effectiveness. Mergers and acquisitions distract them from anything but figuring out how to glue disparate systems together. In most enterprises, they are minding a large legacy system environment and spend about 80 percent of their time and money trying to maintain existing systems, rather than thinking about where the business is going and how they might help. Faced with all these pressures, they lapse back into old approaches or try to find some miraculous and unconventional "solution." All this exacerbates the already broken relationship with business people, and compels business people to look for alternatives that end up weakening the overall effort.

How computers are programmed and how decisions are made about which systems to build, are at the root of the disconnect between business and IT, two vitally important parts of your enterprise. Let's look at how each of them got to where we are today.

How Computer Programming Became A Mess

When computers first began to be used in business, systems were built on programming that was all 0s and 1s. This binary notation represented the instructions for the machine to perform its elementary operations. It was a language for computers, machine language or machine code, by which programmers told the computer's central processing unit to execute this or that task. Numerical machine code of this sort is about as stripped down a language for computers as there is.

This underlying need for translation has remained a constant, for the most part. As new languages came along, with translation still governing the relationship between business people and the machine, the need for specialized skills to program a machine to approximate what business people needed the machine to do grew stronger. The gulf between business and IT widened.

Numerical machine code gave way to assembly code, which eliminated a lot of the tedium of the earlier language, and reduced some of the errors, but did not introduce an actual business language to computer programming. Assembly languages still were translators, taking a series of processor instructions and meta-statements, comments, and data, and translating them into machine language instructions that could be put in a computer's memory and executed.

Things did improve, but only with respect to the languages of the machine themselves, not in bridging that gap between business and IT. Fortran came along in the 1950s, moving programming closer to things that make sense to people by using a more symbolic language. But it was largely for engineers.

Then COBOL arrived, aimed primarily for use in business, finance, and administrative systems and professing to get programming closer to the language of business. COBOL is an acronym for Common Business-Oriented Language—but putting the word "business" into the language's name didn't change things. Business people didn't use COBOL; IT people remained the programmers, and COBOL was still a translation tool.

BASIC arrived, emphasizing ease of use for non-programmers. The acronym stands for Beginner's All-Purpose Symbolic Instruction Code, and the general purpose language did make it possible for some small business owners to create their own small applications on personal computers. But even Business BASIC didn't change that you still had to be a *programmer* to create a system. I had the privilege of learning BASIC at college from its creators Kemeney and Kurtz—but no one ever pretended we were really business-oriented. The language was always viewed from the data structures, the mechanics, and the perspective of the technical implementation.

Along the historical path of computer languages, we eventually got to object-oriented languages. These represent an attempt to abstract a higher order of logic patterns. In object-oriented programming, "objects" are concepts with attributes that describe them (called data fields). Associated procedures are called "methods." Design of applications happens by using the objects to interact with each other.

Fourth-generation programming languages (4GLs), actually packages of systems development software that include programming languages, superseded the third-generation languages (3GLs) that were based more on natural language than ever before, but that were slow and prone to error. Technologists believed that applications could be developed more rapidly if some kind of language and method could just generate the equivalent of 3GLs' instructions, but with fewer errors. Overall, the target was reductions in time, effort and cost to develop systems.

In the history of programming languages, new ones are introduced time and again that are supposed to make it easier for people to program. However, it seems clear that after COBOL and the stated goal of getting closer to business, languages moved in the other direction, away from business. After all, a business programming "language" would not employ the same mental model as traditional programming. Wouldn't it liberate business people from their reliance on specialized programmers holding all the cards in a game of "let's get the needed system built?"

Java is a great example of this move backwards, of a retreat to the orientation of the machine. Its origins can be traced to 1991 under different names. By 1995, Sun Microsystems was releasing its first public implementation, known as Java 1.0. Sun's promise was "Write Once, Run Anywhere" (WORA), and because of this it became very popular. WORA means code that runs on one platform does not need to be recompiled to run on another. It was specifically designed to be general purpose and to have as few implementation dependencies as possible. Pretty soon, it was ubiquitous, with new versions that had multiple configurations built for different types of platforms. Eventually, among young computer geeks, it became *sine qua non* to know Java.

Today, there are millions of Java programmers around the world working for themselves and for companies large and small. Sure, Java is "simpler" or "easier" than many other computer languages in many respects, but the paradigm for Java is still the old one that has kept business and IT people separated, ever since the advent of computing—dedicated programmers are required. For business people, this means they must still go to translators to get their technology needs met. In reality, from a business point of view, COBOL is actually better than Java—though still divorced from the way business people think.

The way computers are programmed, though, is only one of two big disconnects between what business needs and how technology tries to serve those needs. The other disconnect is in how systems development projects are prioritized.

Traditional Development

The lack of understanding about technology on the business side of the enterprise can be illustrated with an analogy. Think of the IT as the architect and the business person as the client who hires the architect to build an addition to her house. The client has a pretty good idea of what she wants. She's been to Home Depot and she reads *House Beautiful* magazine. When it comes to room additions, she's come to understand what is off the shelf, standard, and customized. She knows about bay windows and French doors, and her trips to Home Depot have taught her that door frames are a standard width and that anything else requires extra work and extra money. She also knows there's a standard size for ceiling tiles, which means lots and lots of choices, and that anything other than the standard size will not only increase her costs in the beginning, but make it impossible to take advantage of off-the-shelf options should she choose to change the ceiling tiles sometime in the future.

So, the client and the architect have a very pragmatic discussion. She has a lot to tell him. They discuss not only what the room is for, and how the client wants the room to look, but she is able to stipulate a lot of specific design characteristics. Of course, the architect has opinions, and is certainly capable of introducing alternative ideas, even radical ones. But they talk at a very concrete level about windows and doors and the ceiling and the paint color and so on. The client has been empowered to have that concrete discussion.

Let's contrast this to the typical interaction between business and IT. In the current development model, most of what business people tell IT people is defined abstractly. IT people tell business people not to worry about implementation. With this type of vague interaction at a system's inception, it's no wonder that confusion and miscommunication slip in.

Here's how the traditional development process works in today's typical company. Business people have an idea for how to make things more efficient with customers, or better serve some customer segment, or deal with a new regulation that affects customers. To implement the idea, some kind of new business service based on a software solution is necessary. Business people will have to work with IT.

The process begins with business people writing a requirements document which is supposed to tell IT what the solution must do. The objective is to get *everything* into that document that might matter over the next three to four years, because it's the only chance since it's unlikely there will ever be a version 2 of the system. So, the requirements document becomes an epic act of imagination, a statement of 150 percent of what any business could every possibly need to cover anticipated and imagined needs.

There's also no useful feedback loop; once the IT people get the requirements document, the back-and-forth commences. Eventually, through multiple iterations, the document expresses something everyone believes can actually be developed. So, the IT folks turn around and create design specs.

You'd be hard pressed to find a business or IT person at a company who will tell you that the design specs truly reflect the requirements document, or vice versa. Yet, the former gets turned into code, typically over an extended period of a year or year-and-a-half. The traditional development process is nothing if not slow. By the time users test the application, it corresponds to a customer-related idea that is old itself, and that's a big problem as Gen D barrels down on your business. And, the code is at least three times removed from the original idea. By the time the programs are actually written, they bear little or no resemblance to the original specifications. This is because the traditional development process imposes a gap between how a system is specified, how it is manually programmed, and then again how it is documented. All of this creates a shaky foundation for making any changes, because the poor documentation makes change frightening.

This specification gap plays out commonly in steps. There's a weak blueprint from the outset, so the system developers make poor architectural decisions. Repeated changes in specifications make the blueprint even weaker. As requirements are added to the system and it falls further and further behind schedule, scope creep ensues and the code gets bloated. Often, the final *coup de grâce* is the plan to launch the system with a big bang, switching users virtually overnight, which makes it near impossible to adopt any parts of the system until the whole is "perfect."

Traditional development is sometimes called the "waterfall model." Business people and IT people go through requirements, design, implementation, verification, and end up in maintenance, step-by-step, flowing like water heading down the river —and over the cliff.

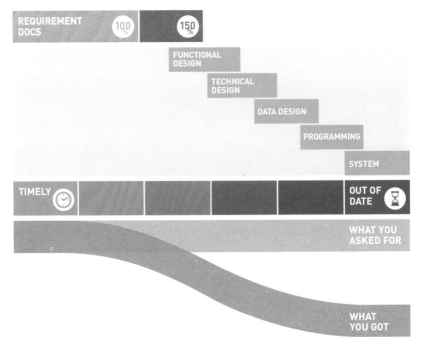

To be sure, the waterfall analogy isn't perfect, but it does highlight many of the issues for concern. Real waterfalls are beautiful. They draw us to them as tourists and delight us when we see them. But the waterfalls of the traditional development process are artificial and rarely do they make anyone smile because it is a process that is highly dysfunctional. For example, the serial nature highlights the lack of feedback, and the eventual deliverable comes crashing, like Niagara Falls, to earth, often with terrifying force and results.

Inevitably, business people are going to need changes that will make the system reflect how they really do business, either because things have changed, or somethings missing, or both. But those changes cost money and time.

All told, the traditional development process creates three fundamental technology problems—stagnant systems, manual systems, and rogue systems— all of which have at their root the simple fact that business people are not getting what they need.

Stagnant Systems

Systems stagnate when business people need changes to them so they can optimize the customer experience, but they can never get those changes implemented. Stagnant systems are an epidemic in the business world. Worse yet, because business people cannot get immediate feedback to learn in real time, stagnate systems also make for stagnate business thinking.

One of the main villains behind stagnant systems is the IT portfolio management process used to allocate scarce capital. It has evolved in concert with (and to help control) the waterfall model. It is analogous to managing an investment portfolio, and there's a good chance your company uses it. The basic idea sounds okay: Determine what to continue investing in versus what to divest from.

Of course, the portfolio management process doesn't solve the long-standing debate on how best to measure the value of an IT investment. Nevertheless, it forces the business side to propose a portfolio of what it wants and needs. From that list, scarce resources are allocated among various parts of the business side (channels, silos, etc.). In essence, competition is created around a culture of scarcity and famine.

The combination of the waterfall and the portfolio management process leads to tight control over demand. You create a dam to manage the flow of those resources, much like creating a reservoir. In that reservoir are all the desires for the technology business people need, analogous to the water held back by the dam. In nature, the water flows continuously over the waterfall, but in the portfolio management process, the water is released selectively, in the form of development projects. The people who control the reservoir have to be convinced to open the sluice gates. Out from the sluice gates of the artificial dam comes whatever project is released, and the water pounds down into the business over the artificially created waterfall. You better have made the right decision before you open those sluice gates.

The portfolio management process is intended to ensure that the most important IT investments are made, but it is enormously frustrating to business people. And it sets up a self-fulfilling prophecy. The portfolio management process, in the context of the traditional development process, drives this culture of over-specification. The entire paradigm is geared to large, overdesigned projects. You propose a big, important-looking system so it will rise to the top. The projects that make it to the top of the list eat up all the available resources, so there's never a chance for a version 2 where you could make important incremental changes that ultimately can drive the very optimized customer experience and efficiency improvements that the system should have addressed in the first place. Without the chance for change, everything stagnates. Knowing that projects always stagnate, business people over specify next time, too, just to try and get as much into the next development process as possible. It's a self-perpetuating reality of system development in business enterprises.

Manual Systems

Next, we come to manual systems, which are efforts to work around stagnant (or even missing) systems. Of course a common reaction to a stagnate system is to "fix" it by adding a manual system. Take credit card disputes. Credit card issuers know that the business rules for disputes has stagnated and is impossible to change, so they simply end up doing dispute manually. Who can blame them? When business people don't get what they need through the traditional development process, they find workarounds. Sometimes, because the expectations of what systems will deliver are so low, business people will even specify things that turn tasks over to people, even though they could be done by the system, just to maintain some ability to change processes without having to reenter the portfolio management process and ask for something new.

Not all manual systems eschew the technology route completely. Some are built around Excel spreadsheets or simple databases, but all have the characteristic of being low-automation. Others are completely manual, implemented through the creation of policies and training rather than using an effective level of automation. Some are combinations of both.

For example, a bank may end up with a stagnant lending system that makes it possible to book loans and do accruals, but provides no guidance to users on the correct credit limit to establish for a given customer, or what the risk consequences to the bank might be of a certain lending decision. So, business users create a manual system as a workaround. But the manual system leaves out critical processes, and people are simply trusted to remember and execute all the right procedures and calculations. It's a potential disaster in the making.

The issues with stagnant systems can actually create an impetus for the introduction of manual systems. Because users are afraid their systems will stagnate, they introduce intermediate manual steps to give themselves a chance to have staff intercede or fix up the parts that haven't evolved with the business need. Indeed, some manual systems are designed for as much human intervention as possible, because the users believe this is the only way to address the fact that needed incremental changes in existing systems are never going to happen. These are vulnerable to error and inconsistency, and even to malicious intent (as you will see in a moment).

Manual systems can be a colossal waste of time, using up human resources that could be so much more effectively employed if people had the right technological tools with which to do their jobs. One example is the "fingernet," which involves toggling between multiple screens on a computer to do work that could be in one screen, if the system had been built correctly, or where a person works on one screen and then swivels his chair around to type some information into another computer.

Another problem is that manual procedures typically leave out lots of the things that ought to be in a real system, like safeguards and controls. The results can be devastating. It was the combination of stagnant systems and manual systems that brought down the venerable Barings Bank in 1995. Trader Nick Leeson was able to game the system, circumventing the bank's internal auditing and risk management controls and ultimately running up losses of $1.4 billion in about a month and a half.

What happened in April and May 2012 at JP Morgan is another story of that same combination of stagnant and manual system resulting in disaster. Transactions booked through the firm's London branch led to massive trading losses. A highly secretive trader named Bruno Iksil, nicknamed "The London Whale," accumulated outsized positions on derivatives known as credit default swaps, and at least $6 billion was lost. Criminal investigations into the firm's risk-management system and internal controls followed.

Fortunately, not all manual systems have these kinds of impacts. Unfortunately, businesses have yet to learn the important lesson they teach: they foster a lack of transparency; they are subject to inconsistent of application of policies and rules; They can make businesses the victims of innocent mistakes or intentional gaming; and they can lead to enormous fines and even the death of a business enterprise.

Rogue Systems

Finally, there are the rogue systems. These are the result of business people, frustrated beyond words, creating well-intentioned but poorly conceived stopgaps to address their needs. They want automation to build processes and rules into their systems. They would prefer to go the mainstream route, but they get caught in the stagnant swamp of the portfolio management process. So they end up, unintentionally, making it difficult to do business well.

Business users who are so desperate and frustrated can end up building huge portfolios of makeshift applications and systems that are completely unsustainable. Make your way through the vast landscape of the business world, and the number of systems you'll see built entirely on complex macros in an Excel spreadsheet will be staggering. The idea that this is the way to optimize the customer experience or intelligently automate operations is laughable, if it weren't so potentially devastating.

Citibank's Global Transaction Services (GTS) division faced this rogue systems problem. GTS provides Citi clients in more than 100 countries with a variety of integrated treasury and trade solutions, along with securities and fund services. These clients are multinational corporations, other financial institutions, and public sector institutions. GTS is supposed to serve local and cross-border interests alike. Today, the service is considered world-class, well-coordinated, and a powerful competitive differentiator. But it wasn't always so.

At one time, Citi GTS operated with little global consistency. There were dozens of baby systems across the globe to track and manage customer service. These systems had grown up over years, as business people—absent being able to get the IT support they wanted and needed—built dozens of them to serve their customers. Some were the result of regional development efforts. Others emerged from "skunk works." Sometimes, they were manual systems using tools such as Excel to maintain this or that list.

Imagine what happened when a huge multinational like Pepsico came to Citi GTS for services, expecting seamlessness and integration. The GTS account manager had no way to get a unified, global picture of Pepsico as a GTS customer. The information was dissipated across many islands of automation. Meanwhile, Pepsico might get a different answer to the same question asked in Detroit and Dubai.

Fortunately, Citi GTS today has all 104 countries on one service backbone, providing overall control to ensure best-in-class service to customers, but with enough flexibility so local offices can do what they need to do that differs from place to place. It was the result of a thoughtful campaign that brought together the right technology and values to convince the individual units how much better life would be for them and their clients with a coherent approach.

Shadow IT

The discipline and teamwork at Citi that brought the groups into alignment is in stark contrast to most companies that have faced the rogue systems problem. In some firms, the creation of and attempts to maintain rogue systems has even become institutionalized, with business people increasingly developing their own systems and solutions without organizational approval, often taking on technology challenges that are well beyond their capacity and leading to disastrous results.

"Business divisions are bypassing the IT department, making their own decisions to buy cloud-based application services or use mobile devices, raising the specter of so-called 'shadow IT' that's outside the knowledge or control of the CIO and the IT staff."[26]

It's unsustainable, and it puts tremendous *bad* pressure on the already tenuous relationship between the business and technology sides of the enterprise. "Now Shadow IT has burst out of the closet and is waltzing around the corporation, leaving IT departments rushing to do damage control." [27]

These Shadow IT systems sometimes don't even have the basic password controls and other things you'd implement in a serious corporate system. Yet, they are used to manage critical aspects of the business—that is, until they break or the "rogues" are caught.

[26] Ellen Messmer, "Does 'shadow IT' lurk in your company?" *NetworkWorld*, August 8, 2012, at www.networkworld.com/news/2012/080812-shadow-it-261502.html
[27] Jill Dyche, "Shadow IT Is Out of the Closet," *Harvard Business Review*, HBR Blog Network, September 13, 2012, at blogs.hbr.org/cs/2012/09/shadow_it_is_out_of_the_closet.html

Mind the Gap?

There are lots of people out there who think they have the answer to how the gap between the great experiences at home and the crappy experiences at work can be bridged. Of the many possible examples, let's just look at one. The Object Management Group (OMG),[28] an international industry consortium founded in 1989, is a not-for-profit group with membership open to any organization, large or small. OMG's mission statement includes "to develop ... integration standards that provide real-world value" and the group's members "share experiences in transitioning to new management and technology approaches like Cloud Computing."

OMG is a good example because of its wide scope. Over the years, OMG task forces have worked on a broad range of technologies and modeling standards, all of which have been touted by various analysts as "next-big-thing" approaches that could solve many of the problems you've read about in the earlier chapters. They run the gamut from "Architecture-Driven Modernization" to "Model-Driven Architecture," from "Real-time, Embedded and Specialized Systems" to the "Unified Modeling Language."

Model-Driven Architecture (MDA) is a big deal to OMG people. It is a software design approach launched by OMG in 2001 that provides a set of guidelines for how to structure specifications, which in MDA are expressed as models. It is supposed to get system design closer to the users, with users abstractly modeling solutions from which an automated tool can derive some or all of the source code necessary for the software system.

[28] See www.omg.org

However, as is pretty typical with gaps, how you think it ought to be addressed can be influenced heavily by which side of the gap you are standing on. OMG stands firmly on the tech side. Thus, the OMG committee that governs MDA conceives of it as a way to define technology, not business. And with its roots in the technical domain, the types of models that cam be designed are aimed at technologists. So, whatever promise it may have, it remains trapped in the old paradigm of technology first. You can be "model driven" while still relying on arcane software code for most of your finished applications.

The Desperation Bandwagon

Out of desperation, businesses are looking for magic bullets and quick fixes to solve their systems problems. One seat on the desperation bandwagon is offshore development. Doing so doesn't solve the fundamental problems that have led to all the bad systems outcomes described earlier. It just moves the problems somewhere else. The only real difference in how your system gets built is that it's being done by people half a world away, most likely in India. Those programmers, though, are still building your system the old-fashioned way, using the traditional development process.

Actually, having huge pools of discounted offshore software coders only makes things worse. When the systems development work is sent offshore, you are exacerbating the dysfunction of an already dysfunctional process. Maybe you're even making the dysfunction come to the fore faster!

Another seat on the desperation bandwagon is cloud computing, the use of hardware and software resources as a service that is delivered over the Internet. It is becoming ubiquitous. You can't watch television for any extended period without seeing some advertisement touting this or that technology, even for businesses, that is "leveraging the power of the cloud." But as is often the case in the hype cycle, this gets teed up to address way more challenges than it effectively can.

Sure, technologically the cloud addresses some of the infrastructure problems enterprises face. It offers a way to reduce friction around deployment and capital expenditures. But in terms of changing the way your systems are *built*, the cloud offers nothing. And something those ads don't mention is that when you use the cloud, you are entrusting your data, software, and computation to some remote service.

Still, the cloud is a big part of Gen D's online world. So, a lot of those who sell business technology like to present cloud computing as doing what the cool kids are doing. That's why so much new development at companies today is focused on iPads and Facebook and Twitter. And that's why a growing number of your employees are probably bringing their own devices and software to work. You've probably seen this trend unfold, especially with younger employees, as they try to bridge the gap by using their own tools, the ones with which they've long been satisfied.

Could the cloud and commoditized software offered as a service possibly substitute for customer processes like those described in Chapter 4? Would you put your memory and judgment and muscle into someone else's *generic* body, and expect it to function in a way that serves your interests best? Of course not. The thought that you could do so and have it best serve your customers' intent is ludicrous.

At a more technical level, you face immense challenges integrating cloud services with your existing systems. Trying to achieve the heavy degree of customization you'd need even to approach genuine customer processes would be considerably more expensive than anything your IT people might build from scratch. So, while the cloud may address some infrastructure and support problems, it doesn't even *begin* to help you answer this question: What does the cloud do to help make me special to my customers?

If that doesn't convince you, along come "rogue clouds." Indeed, the cloud is now the breeding ground for the next generation of rogue systems—hacked together and suffering from poor maintainability and stagnation. Fortune 500 computer security software company Symantec conducted a global survey and reported in early 2013 that a huge majority of businesses are seeing costs rise from "rogue cloud implementations."[29] These rogue cloud implementations take the form of business people implementing public cloud applications that no one on the IT side of the enterprise manages, integrates into the company's IT infrastructure, or—in many cases—*even knows about!*

Beyond the costs, the security issues are monumental.

"So why are organizations doing it?" the report asks. "One in five don't realize they shouldn't. However, the most commonly cited reason for these rogue cloud projects was to save time and money: Going through IT would make the process more difficult."

So, before you even have a chance to fight off Gen D's efforts to kill your business, your own people might help your business commit suicide.

---

[29] Symantec, "Avoiding the Hidden Costs of the Cloud," 2013, at www.symantec.com/content/en/us/about/media/pdfs/b-state-of-cloud-global-results-2013.en-us.pdf

Agile Programming to the Rescue?

Some alternatives have been put forward to solve the problems of the traditional development process and the stagnant, manual, and rogue systems to which it leads. One of them is "agile software development." It's helpful, to a degree, but it's also inadequate.

First introduced in the 2001 "Manifesto for Agile Software Development,"[30] it is based on an iterative and incremental development model in which requirements and solutions are meant to evolve. The process is collaborative, meant to involve cross-functional teams that organize themselves to get the work done. As such, it is quite different from the relationship described earlier between business and IT people, and much closer to that of the architect and client. It goes in the right direction.

However, agile development doesn't solve the fundamental problems. Too often, agile development projects are still subject to the portfolio management process, which means the selection process will still preclude "version 2" and beyond. It continues to subject business users with an overly burdensome specifications activity that ultimately leads them to the same old inflexible and non-evolving systems you get from traditional development. In other words, "agile" in a waterfall culture becomes stagnant. You just get to stagnant systems faster. What you really need is agile development in an agile culture.

This is why even in organizations that have adopted agile programming to a significant degree, business people still create a lot of manual systems.

Ready to Change?

Organizational managers have known for years that there are far too many holes in the ways they control processes, and the judgment and risk built into those processes. Unfortunately, they have had little choice but to go along with manual processes or semi-automated, disjointed rogue systems simply because to do otherwise would likely grind business to a halt. When business people undertake projects that end up as manual and rogue systems, they institutionalize gaps in the processes and controls across *entire* companies. Yes, they are just trying to find a way to get their work done, but they don't necessarily create systems that incorporate sound business judgment. The consequences can be far greater than missing some new business opportunity. In fact, as the Barings Bank and JP Morgan examples illustrate, they can be catastrophic.

---

[30] The manifesto comprises only a few lines of text and may be read at http://agilemanifesto.org

It's not hard to fathom why these systems emerge, especially when you consider that business people and IT people have been working at what seems to be cross-purposes for so long, and that often they seem incapable of communicating effectively. Meanwhile, the IT people can't support and maintain all this stuff, get angry at business people, and the cycle of fighting over control goes on and on. Maybe IT makes a knee-jerk promise to standardize things, playing to the lowest common denominator among its internal customers. And with systems they build, they ask for requirements from the ultimate users, but they never iterate with their internal customers and let them in on the process.

So, what do you do? MDA, the cloud, just about every "solution" described earlier is a placebo. And while the sentiment to replicate at work the positive experiences people have with their home devices is a worthy one, home technology is not the path to genuine business technology. The reason is simple: The design for home technology, all those things that begin with "i," is geared to the individual. That's completely reasonable, but it cannot substitute for business technology. In a business setting, technology should no more be organized around the IT people than it should organized around the *individual* business person.

As laid out at the beginning of this chapter, your starting point for optimizing the customer experience and intelligently automating operations, for bringing your customers into high-definition, is to change how everyone in your organization thinks about technology. It's the precursor to changing how you create and use systems. Clearly, the traditional development approach that led you into stagnant, manual, and rogue systems has to go. You have to ditch those requirements and design specs that are part of the waterfall model. You need a rational approach to the totality of your technology, driven by business decisions and not by the individual and highly controlled "sluice gate" mentality. You have to change the collaboration model between your business and IT people, so that systems are being built based on the language of business, defined by the people who will use them and who will interact with your customers. Ultimately, everything must be about the customer. If you don't understand that, you will never achieve 1080.

The technology you need to embrace is something that can make it possible to combine the data 360, intent 360, and customer processes 360 and get them working together as 1080.

And yet, even with all that, you cannot rely only on changing things about the technology. Technology is more important than ever before because of the digital environment that breeds Gen D expectations and assumptions, but it is not the only imperative when it comes to preparing for the customerpocalypse. You need to change your organization, too, liberating it from the shackles of old thinking and old models. Let's look at how.

CHAPTER 6

Liberating Your Organization

When a leading benefits management company in the United States began to bring its customers into 1080 high-definition, the senior leadership quickly realized that it needed to completely rethink how it organized, hired, trained and rewarded its people as part of an entirely new way of doing business. The company established a radically new organizational structure better suited to close collaboration with its connected customer base and enhancing the customer experience. Its model is a good one for other businesses to adopt.

Just as with changing the relationship between business and IT, an organization that wants to enter this 1080 high-def world has no choice but to change its structure. But it's not enough simply to shift things around on the organizational chart. There also has to be a culture change, because as the management consultant and author Peter Drucker famously said: "Culture eats strategy for breakfast."

How do you get there? One step involves fundamentally changing the relationship between business and IT in your organization. It stands to reason that if you're going to undertake the kind of transformation discussed in Chapter 4 with respect to how technology is thought of, developed, and used, that relationship is going to have to undergo some serious changes.

Hybrid Vigor for Business and IT

Lots of enterprises make organizational changes that affect how business and IT people interact, sometimes even aligning their reporting within the company. But to transform that relationship in the context of becoming Gen D friendly, a customer-centric, high-def organization, you have to go even further and align the two in new ways. One approach to achieving that objective is to cross-pollinate, just like in the plant world.

Cross-pollination occurs when pollen is delivered to a flower from a different plant. Most plants have adapted to reproducing through cross-pollination, and the plant world has developed a host of mechanisms to maximize this virtuous circle of fertilization and reproduction.

What makes cross-pollination a good thing? The answer is simple: You combine the best "pieces" of DNA from multiple sources to create a strong new whole.

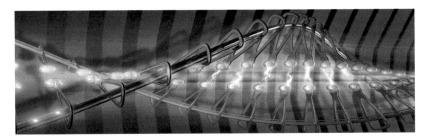

Enterprises can benefit from the same concept, and cross-pollination's praises have been sung in the business world for some time. "Cross-pollination is big these days. Whether you're a retailer or a research lab, the gospel is that if you mix things up you'll get a creative ferment," wrote Lee Fleming in a decade-old *Harvard Business Review* article.[31]

I suggest going even further. Consider one of the benefits of cross-pollination that leads to something truly transformative—*heterosis or hybrid vigor*, the improved or increased vigor or other superior qualities that arise when genetically different plants or animals are crossbred. Heterosis is the term used to describe this phenomenon when the parents are taken from different populations of the same species, while hybrid vigor is used when the parents come from different species. You may argue that business people and IT people are just different populations of the same species, but decades of observation suggest that hybrid vigor is the appropriate term here.

For instance, the benefits management company mentioned at the top of this chapter undertook a major cross-pollination effort that included a massive revamp of its organizational structure. Hundreds of employees were pulled out of the IT organization to help populate a new world. They were sent to work directly with the business lines as part of "innovation centers." Management created a healthy and competitive innovation incubator that rewarded the right kind of investments in projects to enhance the customer experience. Funding and incentives were tied to these projects' success in generating real business results within a short period, typically a financial quarter.

---

[31] Lee Fleming, "Perfecting Cross-Pollination," Harvard Business Review, September 2004.

The innovation centers were supported in turn by business process centers that ensured consistent and excellent processes across all channels. Of course, IT continued to support the horizontal plumbing needed by the innovation teams to get their jobs done, but without distracting them from their critical customer-facing processes.

This all resulted in a form of hybrid vigor. In the new environment, behaviors and expectations changed. Business and IT people working together in the innovation centers began to pull together in ways they had never done before. They saw themselves as part of a team, not as users and providers of a service. The cross-pollination began work to change the mindset and culture of the business and IT people, which was then reinforced with an organizational change.

Over time, the business and IT people in the innovation centers underwent a radical shift, together. They became like the architect and homeowner client of Chapter 5. The architect brought technical knowledge to the discussion, and the client was fully empowered to have a concrete discussion about the technology.

It's like a matrix, but goes even further. Common processes were defined across business lines. Then whatever could be standardized and synthesized was done, while individual lines of business were still allowed to set out on their own in cases where that was necessary. By serving customers uniformly, the customer experience is always in high-def. The common framework for common business processes made the business agile and adaptable, and the management structure reflected these characteristics. The IT people maintained an architecture that is manageable, predictable, and logical. And the management structure supported this, too.

The COO at the time said that the organizational shift to innovation centers dramatically reduced operating expenses, thanks to the redesign of the core processes. He also described all the cash it generated over time. The projected 30-percent productivity gain over 10 years created a tremendously high return on invested capital.

ING Poland has realized tremendous benefits, too. As part of a strategic initiative to modernize its sales and distribution capabilities, the company set out to standardize and merge individual processes in a way that brought together best practices. Thanks to the effort, the captive agent sales force (those selling only ING products) was completely modernized. Agents could be up and running, selling to customers, within eight weeks when it had taken six months before the initiative. ING Poland extended its market leadership by expanding into new sales areas, new geographies and markets across Eastern Europe, with new products and opening up new distribution channels, all of which took advantage of commonalities in processes. The achievement of 80 percent reuse of processes was a phenomenal statistic.

Break the Grips of Channels and Silos

Your organization doesn't need to follow exactly the same path to cross-pollination. There are a few guiding principles to follow, and then you can construct the solution that makes the most sense for your particular circumstance. Look at the opportunities in your enterprise. What is common but isn't organized with commonality in mind? What can be made common? Build on that. Find everything that can be done in common across channels, silos, departments, and so on. It's the beginning of "layer-cake" thinking. You do this by identifying everything from the customer perspective. And you look for things that seem to have, or sound like they have, similar attributes. Inevitably, they've been cobbled together in individual silos.

This can be more difficult than it may seem. Typically, when enterprises try to plan for reuse and shared processes, the entrenched organizations within the enterprise insist that everything they do is unique and has little or nothing in common with other departments or lines of business. That's rarely the case.

"We had a group of people on the clinical side come together a little while ago, and they all thought that they did a certain piece of work very differently," says a senior IT leader at a top-five U.S. healthcare organization. "When you peeled away the onion back, they were all doing pretty much the same thing, but there was this 5 percent of difference in the processes."[32]

Those differences, she continued, "were more around the regional or localities that they were operating in ... If you understand that those are the things that are different, those are the things you can start to build into your model."

With that understanding, you can make it possible for every channel, silo, and department to snap into core processes and vice versa. This is the third of the 360s that make up 1080 customer high-def. If a channel has an order processing issue, there should be only one place to go to get it addressed, and it needs to be addressed in a way that crosses every vertical line in the organizational structure.

Create New Executive Coordination Roles

Some organizations have gone even further, establishing a new executive position called chief process officer (CPO). This is recognition of just how important it is to elevate the visibility of and attention to critical customer pro-

---

[32] Carole Rizzo, former chief information officer of Kaiser Permanente, speaking at PegaWORLD 2008, Washington, D.C.

cesses throughout the enterprise. In large part, it is geared to the idea that as the business goes to market in whatever vertical setting, the correct horizontal leverage points have been uncovered and are being put to effective use.

There's also a chief customer officer (CCO) role emerging. Forrester analysts Harley Manning and Paul Hagen, for example, have taken note of the growing number of enterprises that have made an organizational commitment to putting the customer into high-definition by establishing this position. They mention EMEX, Fidelity, Boeing, Charter, General Motors, Maersk Line, and The Washington Post. In his book with Kerry Bodine, Manning explains how CCOs may range from playing a purely advisory role, to a matrixed role across functional roles, to being given full operational authority.[33]

Most CCOs, it turns out, are former division presidents or general managers or come from the marketing, sales, or operations organizations. That some are maturing into roles with wide, direct operational oversight is a sign of the times.

Redesign the Role of Customer Service

You'll also need to determine just how you're going to match customer intentions with business intent and based on that, define new roles for customer service. This is a major undertaking. The model of customer service that will correspond to what Gen D demands bears little resemblance to how the overwhelming majority of businesses do customer service now. But the fact is that no enterprise can move its customers to 1080 high-definition if it is stuck in the past. The change begins with throwing out the old definitions.

Consider some of those old, traditional definitions online. Think about these in the context of what you now know about enhancing the customer experience to bring customers into high-definition, and what it might mean for people in your enterprise who interact with customers.

Customer service, says businessdictionary.com, is "All interactions between a customer and product provider at the time of sale, and thereafter. Customer service adds value to product and builds enduring relationships."[34] Investopedia puts it this way: "The process of ensuring customer satisfaction with a product or service. Often, customer service takes place while performing a transaction for the customer, such as making a sale or returning an item. Customer service can take the form of an in-person interaction, a phone call, self-service systems, or by other means."[35]

---

[33] Harley Manning and Kerry Bodine, *Outside In: The Power of Putting Customers at the Center of Your Business,* Boston, Mass.: New Harvest, 2012.

[34] At www.businessdictionary.com/definition/customer-service.html

[35] At www.investopedia.com/terms/c/customer-service.asp#axzz2IvkyuY4e

Wikipedia's article on the topic turns to a textbook for its definition. "Customer service is a series of activities designed to enhance the level of customer satisfaction—that is, the feeling that a product or service has met the customer expectation."[36]

Are you noticing anything common to these definitions? There's "time of sale, and thereafter." Then there's "satisfaction with a product or service" and "while performing a transaction … such as a sale …" These are all transactional definitions, and they assume—indeed, kick in—only when the customer is, presumably, about to hand over some money.

With its focus on excellence, BizWatch Online takes a slightly different approach: "Excellent customer service is the process by which your organization delivers its services or products in a way that allows the customer to access them in the most efficient, fair, cost effective, and humanly satisfying and pleasurable manner possible."[37] Still, though, it's linked to a transaction. So far, we haven't seen a word about a customer relationship, let alone one that can last a lifetime.

When your customers are in 1080 high-definition, you will have transactions with them, of course. But it's not those transactions that will guide how you organize to interact with your customers and how the interactions actually unfold. Rather, it will be the relationships you build with your customers, which will be built on the three 360 elements of 1080, data, intent, and processes, along with the overarching objective of enhancing the customer experience. To get there, you have no choice but to throw out every transaction-centered definition of what customer service is. In fact, you need to drop the antiquated idea of customer "service" altogether.

That's what American Express did, taking its organization through a transformation of its old customer service model and emerging with redefined roles for its customer service representatives. Those who embraced the change, along with new hires, became Customer Care Professionals responsible for customer *engagement*. Entrenched, backward-thinking customer service reps who couldn't make the shift to doing business in the new way were let go.

Consider the difference between those two words, service and engagement. Let's focus on their verb forms. To engage is to occupy, attract, or involve someone's interest or attention; or to cause someone to become involved in something, such as a conversation or discussion or relationship. Many of us were *engaged* to (with) our future spouses. *Engagement* is a word of relationship.

---

[36] Efraim Turban *et al., Electronic Commerce 2002: A Managerial Perspective*, 2nd ed., Upper Saddle River, N.J.: Prentice-Hall, 2002.
[37] Jack Speer, "What Is the Definition of Customer Service?," BizWatch Online, at www.bizwatchonline.com/BWJuly06/article3_0904.htm

By contrast, to service (in the customer service context) is to perform business functions that are auxiliary to production or distribution of something. That's not a word of relationship.

American Express set out to change its interactions with customers from service to engagement, a people business that builds relationships. The transformation began with an operating framework based on what Jim Bush, executive vice president of World Service for AmEx, calls a simple concept: Enable, engage, and empower. The enable part has been to create a global, integrated delivery of a promise to customers that their experience with American Express would be superb, and fulfill that promise by leveraging technology, people inside the company, and their passion. It was, and continues to be a challenge to get everyone on the same page, especially to understand that the old silo view of customer service had to be abandoned in favor of something that fits with the cross-organizational experience against which customers measure their experience with American Express.

Engage means putting the customer first, and understanding *how* to engage. As Bush tells it, this is all about listening to the customer's voice and changing the business model for American Express to reflect what the customer is saying. The new measure for the company became the straightforward Net Promoter question: "Would you recommend American Express to a friend?"

The Net Promoter question comes from Fred Reichheld in his book *The Ultimate Question 2.0*.[38] Reichheld details how some customers are promoters and others are detractors. An American Express customer who answers yes to the question above is a promoter.

Several industries have dismally low average "Net Promoter Scores," a sign to me of the profound failure of companies to deal well with customers across the board, and particularly with younger customers from whom they face the wrath of an outright revolt against the old ways of doing business. In descending order, from bad to worse, these industries are cellular phone service, banks, airlines, credit cards, life insurance, health insurance, Internet, cable and satellite TV. Those last three have *negative* scores. American Express was determined not to be among those failures.

The third part of Jim Bush's operating framework, empower, is about unleashing the abilities of American Express people who are in direct contact with customers to connect and build relationships. The company figured out how to unleash the personalities of their people, to let them be themselves, and make that come through with customers so that engagement was something real, something person-to-person and not

---

[38] Fred Reichheld (with Rob Markey), *The Ultimate Question 2.0: How Net Promoter Companies Thrive in a Customer-Driven World*, Boston: Harvard Business Review Press, 2011.

customer-to-service rep. This wasn't easy, and American Express had to change its recruitment model for its Customer Care Professionals. Focused around the concept of extraordinary service, American Express cycled out "bad-attitude" customer service reps, recruiting "hospitable" people, changing compensation, and rewarding people not on the old-fashioned metric of average handle time, but on a new concept Bush calls "customer handling time." He defines it as an amount of time the customer dictates, based on what the customer wants and needs. That, ultimately, drives customer satisfaction. Training Customer Care Professionals changed, too. What had once been 70 to 80 percent of training spent on technical stuff flipped completely, to 70 to 80 percent spent on how to treat people and engage with customers as people. All of this has enabled American Express to live by its own golden rule: Treat the customer as you would like to be treated.

Rewire the CFO Function

One of the most significant changes your organization needs to make has to do with your chief financial officer. That's because transforming an entire organization, creating a new relationship between business and IT, and bringing your customers into high-definition is going to require making investments in people and technology. That's going to catch the attention of your chief financial officer—as well it should. The CFO is going to ask the traditional finance questions about return on investment: How long does it take? How much does it cost? What exactly are we getting for that money?

There's nothing intrinsically wrong with these questions, but the measures a CFO typically uses to answer them are problematic. How so? The CFO is traditionally linked to the way waterfall development unfolds and how the portfolio management process is used, as described in Chapter 5. That means the CFO treats building software and using technology as if you were building a huge factory. You typically can't move in until the entire house is completed. But when you're architecting pieces of a good system, with business people and IT people collaborating to meet business needs, you should be able to build those pieces to deploy "one room at a time."

That is completely foreign to the way the CFO sees capital investments and thus to the questions the CFO asks. The CFO wants to know the entire plan up front, which in the traditional development process may actually mean after 20 to 30 percent of the project costs have already been incurred. Typically, organizations use seed funding or have IT people do things "off the books" to get to a point where they can answer the questions in a way the CFO can accept. All this can end up reinforcing the waterfall approach precisely because the additional preparation makes it more likely the project will survive the gauntlet of the portfolio management process.

If you abandon the waterfall model and the portfolio management process, you also have to change how you measure the investment. Otherwise, the answers the CFO gets are not going to bode well for moving forward.

The solution lies in changing the CFO's perspective. Instead of insisting on all the facts up front, CFOs need to see that the path to monitoring the investment in business technology involves making directionally correct decisions supplemented with feedback loops and validated by intermediate results. In other words, keep track of the financial side, but recognize that business people are going to live in some rooms before the house is finished, and that they may even redecorate those rooms along the way.

It can be done. You need to move your CFO to this new perspective. What does the CFO need to do? He or she needs to go from today's highly planned model for making decisions about technology investments to a model that is more iterative and experientially based, wherever that makes sense. It's close-order inspection as an alternative to planning. The CFO also needs to accept development projects being done in a way that makes them easy to launch with methods to determine what the project's real capabilities are before full commitments are made. This means a change in the mindset about hurdle rates and return-on-investment calculations.

A radical model for this comes to us from Janette Sadik-Khan, a commissioner of the New York City Department of Transportation who was previously senior vice president at the engineering firm Parsons Brinckerhoff. Her current work focuses on the design of cities and city streets. In an article for *Bloomberg Businessweek,* Sadik-Khan described the kind of empirical, experiential approach advocated here.

"One of our greatest innovations is our ability to move quickly. The normal capital construction program takes about five years. But we've been able to transform city streets virtually overnight. You can literally paint the city you want to see. You can do it with two traffic cones, a can of paint, and stone planters. And we're able to show the results."[39]

Imagine the ability to do that with systems for your up-and-coming Gen D customers.

---

[39] Janette Sadik-Khan, "The Benefits of a Well-Designed City," *Bloomberg Businessweek,* January 24, 2013, at http://www.businessweek.com/articles/2013-01-24/janette-sadik-khan-the-benefits-of-a-well-designed-city (accessed February 2, 2013).

It is possible. With tight interval control, you and your CFO can get the assurances that outcomes of a given development project will be good or that it can be stopped before everyone is too far into it. Of course, it will make a big difference if the technology being developed is, first and foremost, a way to optimize the customer experience and intelligently automate operations. If the CFO has been converted to the concept of transforming from IT to business technology, this will be much, much easier.

Increasingly, CFOs are becoming thought leaders in organizations. This is reinforced by a growing number of operational people being named CFOs, rather than old school accountants and finance people. More big companies have CFOs with operating experience than ever before.

That means CFOs are bringing a different skill set to the table. They can take that skill set and put it to use to change the way the systems development cycle begins. This may be more important than anything the chief information officer might do in this regard.

What can make all this feasible is the subject of our next chapter.

CHAPTER 7

Staying Alive

The first chapter of this book posed a set of questions:
- Is your company prepared for the demographic reality barreling down on you like a runaway train, driven by new digital technologies?
- Is your company prepared for the Gen D future, or is it on life support?
- Are you ready to make dramatic changes in how you think about customers and customer engagement to ensure the continuity of your business?
- Will you commit to doing everything necessary to keep customers from hating your business and some from possibly trying to kill it?

In examples from Prudential, American Express, OCBC, and other companies, you've seen bits and pieces, some of them very large, of the changes businesses are making as they prepare for Gen D. The examples illustrate how a fundamental shift in the mindset about how technology must support business, coupled with the 1080 high-definition customer view made possible by the data-intent-customer process combination, is the start of the path to staying alive.

The companies you've read about are letting the business drive the technology. They are empowering business people in their organizations and re-positioning technology to serve customer interests. None of them have completely transformed every aspect of what they do to prepare for the new Gen D world, but they are probably way ahead of your business.

In Chapter 3, you read about OCBC's intent-driven process for engaging customers in opening new accounts. As exemplary as that may be, it's still "old school" from a Gen D perspective. But OCBC has a very clear picture of the Gen D train barreling down the tracks. So, OCBC has introduced FRANK.

Mind you, OCBC is no fly-by-night banking upstart. It is a $200 billion financial institution that already controls more than a quarter of the total youth market in Singapore. But the company is committed to locking in Gen D customers by doing business in a way that doesn't seem like business, instead letting customers *discover* the bank.

The FRANK name comes from the phrase "frankly speaking," a reflection of OCBC's understanding that Gen D expects honesty, transparency and sincerity. The brick-and-mortar FRANK stores—and they are stores, not what you typically think of as bank branches—seem to have been modeled after the Apple store. Young people are drawn into the stores, which are located in malls where Gen D hangs out. The objective of the store design is to encourage customers to browse, touch, and ask questions. Yes, touch, just as if you were shopping for clothes or some kind of gadget.

The FRANK website looks like the website for Virgin Mobile, a cellphone provider geared to young customers, but with anything looking business-like stripped down to the bare essentials.[40] The bank made a conscious decision to omit anything even remotely superfluous. For instance, there isn't even the ubiquitous link to an "About Us" page. Products are minimal, and cross-promotion is king. Apply for a tuition loan and you get a gift voucher for the movies. Open a checking account and you get a laptop sleeve. If you can convince four friends to sign up for FRANK products, you'll all share in $50 worth of Ben & Jerry's ice cream.

OCBC offers higher-than-normal interest rates to FRANK customers who open savings accounts, and fuels their loyalty with a "savings enabler" tool that allows them to create sub-accounts in the form of "savings jars" that they name themselves, just like putting change into a jar at home. And that money can't be accessed through an ATM.

Core Principles for Survival

How did OCBC get to the point where the company could see clearly down those tracks and know what to do to prepare? The bank has been working on liberating its organization, just as I described in Chapter 6, and it has changed the way business people and technology people interact in the organization. OCBC is also putting technology to use in a new way, which, when teased apart, reveals three core principles that make feasible everything you've read about up to this point.

- Democratize how you do technology.
- Think in layers.
- Use analytics to optimize continually.

Each principal has a business component and a technology component, but is fundamentally about making technology empower and serve the business people in your organization. Technology is at the center of your ability to respond to the Gen D threat.

---

[40] www.frankbyocbc.com/

Democratize How You Do Technology

When people first began to create documents, it was an arduous and individual task that involved chiseling stone, which gave way to writing on parchment. The individual nature of the process changed when groups of scribes collaborated to create great tomes, usually of religious works. Along came the printing press, a new technology that democratized the creation and dissemination of documents by making it possible for you to hand over what you wrote to someone who could mass produce copies of your document.

Much later, the typewriter came along. Individual writers shifted to the new technology. Businesses created typing pools. Large companies had huge typing pools, often floors and floors of mostly women who would type up handwritten notes from the men of the company or turn Dictaphone loops into documents. When Wang Laboratories invented dedicated word processing computers, all those typing scribes were empowered with new technology.

The next step in democratization, the personal computer, arrived. It directly empowered people at all levels to take direct control—wiping out the typing pools. With personal computers, business people could be their own typing pools.

Now, information technology has caught up with writing and publishing—empowering changed relationships between business and IT and unleashing a new wave of automation. Not only is *access* to technology more democratic, but there now exists the ability to shift the control of, responsibility over, and accountability for technology away from dedicated gurus and experts with some mysterious and impenetrable skill set to business people operating more centrally within their domain of knowledge and using the language and metaphors of business to guide how technology gets used. It is a complete reversal from IT driving the use of technology to business people driving its use.

In simple terms, this means you, the business person, no longer need visit the technology wizard to make a simple, but important change to a business system. The wizards only need to engage in the rarest of circumstances, leaving them to concentrate on where they can add the greatest value implementing the most technically complex or extreme systems for analysis or transaction. Even for word processing, nearly all that can be done by business people themselves, and the wizards—in this case, professional designers and creative document experts—are only needed for certain special published communication.

Democratizing how we do technology means dramatically shifting the power base within your organization. It is about getting rid of technology language in favor of business language and actuating organizational liberation. Business people no longer need technology translators, despite that translation may well be what most IT people continue to do. Today's powerful computers make it possible to move from having to use machine language to being able to use direct business language. And if a computer can be programmed with direct business language, it stands to reason that a business person can do that work directly, eliminating the murkiness and misunderstanding that can occur when translation must be done.

Think In Layers

What happens when you've empowered your business people to drive technology, not the other way around, is that they themselves can build solutions that are much more likely to correspond to the real needs of your customers. The technologists who have been creating your systems have been coerced by the toolsets they use to create systems that are flat. These systems, because they are constrained by the rigid computer codes and language described in Chapter 5, cannot possibly serve more than two layers or dimensions.

However, your business clearly has *more* than two layers and, indeed, has multiple aspects and dimensions. Business problems, decisions, issues, processes, and customers are multidimensional. And your nascent Gen D customers have layers of situation, circumstance, and context that are exponentially more complex than we can even imagine.

Looking across industries, it becomes apparent that the differences within given businesses fall within a fairly consistent set of dimensions. They are *customers, products*, and *jurisdictions*. Customers may be of different types. Products fall into different categories. Jurisdictions, usually geographic, impose different rules, regulations, and culture-driven ways of doing business and dealing with customers.

This brings us to the second core principle, think in layers. First and foremost, layers require that your technology be able to work across multiple customers, products, and jurisdictions in ways that correspond to the multiple aspects of your customers. The binary, if-then, two-layer systems you now have create some very bad choices for you when you try to think in the rich multidimensional world of your customer. Actually, bad doesn't even come close—the choices are *horrible*.

Imagine you're a bank with a system that can write loans in North America, where there are particular rules and regulations, customer types, and even business intent specific to that part of the world. You expand to England, and you want to use that same system to write loans there. But wait! That system has all sorts of manual connections linked to specifically North American criteria. So, to adapt the system, you need to look at all of its 500+ system modules, and then manually identify the 35 or so that need to be changed in some way.

Here's your first horrible choice: Make each of those separate modules more complicated so they can handle both North America and England. You do this by creating new code branches, using if-then-else constructs. Or you create an unsustainable and ever-growing mass of many little decisions for the system to use to differentiate effectively between North America and England.

You have created a monster. The differences between North America and England are now spread across 35 versions or modules. What happens when your bank expands to Spain and Portugal? The conditionalization becomes more and more complex, until you get to the point where it's very dangerous to make changes. For instance, you might create the very real possibility that when your success leads to opening branches in Brazil, making changes to accommodate that new business opportunity could break the system for use in England. That's because everything is linked together into a horrible series of decisions that makes no real sense.

The problem with creating different modules and "versions" specific to different conditions or location is that every conceivable circumstance must be known ahead of time. In other words, the world is not allowed to change.

The second, even more horrible, choice involves copying the original 35 system modules and then changing or deleting whatever you need to so they work for England. The advantage is that now England and North

America have exactly what they need. There's no extra overhead, and no extra processing, but neither is there any sharing or re-use. But again, England is spread across 35 modules. You have two versions of the same underlying piece of code that are probably no more than five percent different. What happens when you expand again, and eventually you've done this seven more times? Maybe it's a different five percent that needs to change. Will you ever be able to find all the relevant things to change? Not to mention that you have to test the other 95 percent in every version of the system to make sure you haven't introduced any new problems.

With either choice, the next thing you know is that your linear system is a massive, unsupportable mess. In fact, you have multiple messes—called "versions." Want to find out what's happening in Germany? Forget it, unless you're willing to devote a lot of resources to scouring all of the incredibly messy systems.

Both of these choices lead to stagnant systems, and both business and IT people say they simply don't know what the systems actually do. Those stagnant systems encourage manual systems and rogue systems, because business people need to get their work done.

The critically necessary alternative is to think in layers. Identifying what's common and what's distinctive. Figure out the degrees of difference. Tell the computer, in simple terms, what you've found. The modern computer, fully capable of fulfilling this function for you, can then simply give you the multidimensional technology tool you need.

Once you've gotten past the restraints of traditional programming language and you've empowered business people by democratizing how you do technology, thinking in layers becomes easier. You can build systems with layers that eliminate the horrible choices. It will be as easy as having business people simply specify what's different between North America and England and let the computer do the rest. The business people will be able to make simple adjustments for a particular customer or class of customers, particular products, particular geographies, particular channels ... you name it.

Today's computers will take care of the rest. They are fully capable of writing their own code, the way they do in the 4GLs described in Chapter 5. Software can now understand what business people have to say, in their own language, and can go directly from model to an actual, usable system with full functionality. You bypass the arcane practice of coding and go directly to building what your business people need.

A useful, if simplistic visualization, for this layered approach comes from the world of digital media and the way in which designers use composite layers to create different versions of images and movies. Designers can choose what is unique and specific, without sacrificing inheritance from their parent layers. Different layers can be turned off and on within the same artwork to create different results for different purposes. Today's digital artists, unlike today's computer software programmers, do not need to make multiple "branched" versions of a file that force them to create completely new versions manually.

In the following Adobe Photoshop example, the designer has deselected the eyeball on the left so that the US and UK layers and bronze customers will not show up in this composite—just the ones we want for our purposes at the moment, only the gold customers in Canada. Our business systems should be this easy.

Unfortunately, the problem of not thinking in layers is endemic across the computing landscape. It isn't being addressed in the shadow IT organizations, and does not go away when you move to the cloud. Businesses using the cloud still remain dependent on the technologists for the solutions themselves. Someone still has to write code to make business logic changes to reflect new products, new procedures, new regulations and new customer behaviors. But code is the status quo and that means code just gets in the way of efficient business.

The good news is there's simply no longer a need to rely on writing code. Business people today can illustrate their processes, think in layers, set their goals, and then state unequivocally to the computer what constitutes a proper outcome. Then they can let the computer do the work.

Use Analytics to Optimize Continually

Once you have begun to think in layers, across many dimensions, and your technology thinks the same way, you can further empower your business people so they can continuously refine your high-definition view of customers. This is critical preparation for the coming Gen D customerpocalypse. Analytics allow you to validate and further tease apart the dimensionality, giving credibility to your own multidimensional thinking. Analytics help you determine whether you've identified the right dimensions for the right customers. From analytics, you get extra insight.

Chapter 3 describes the approach called *next-best-action* that allows you to use advanced analytics to examine trends and patterns across millions of customers. These dynamic analytics are a way to sense customer needs, choices, preferences, and how to anticipate behavior. And they are at the heart of the third core principle for achieving genuine business technology.

Dynamic analytics are a prerequisite to keeping your customer in sharp focus. During an interaction with a customer, you or the customer can add new data that can dynamically change the results from the underlying predictive model. Imagine a customer interacting with a financial institution, and the institution finds out during the interaction that the customer has just inherited $500,000 from a deceased relative. This would dramatically change the risk score of the customer. The system adapts so that the customer's choices change to whatever the institution has decided in advance is more appropriate for a customer fitting the new profile. In other words, dynamic analytics make that intent 360 possible.

But it is also goes beyond the data—the very path through the system provides input to the customer's level of interest. This is as true in a guided interaction (say, with a contact center) as it is in looking at how a customer navigates a website during self-service.

Humans adapt to other humans all the time, in real time. That's the very nature of human interaction, as information is provided back and forth between two or more people. Why shouldn't technology do the same?

Rob Walker, the colleague who provided the C.C. Sabathia baseball analogy in Chapter 3, imagined "unleashing" predictive, dynamic analytics on healthcare data. Consider just a few of his examples of how it might be used in that domain, and then imagine how powerful it would be in getting to true business technology. He suggests its employment to predict the duration of operations, pre- and peri-operative complications from surgery, transplant rejection, complications in newborn babies, and so on. In the case of predicting post-operative atrium arrhythmia, the tool would identify when and which additional medications are necessary during procedures to ensure better outcomes. He also showed how scheduling based on predictive duration of operations would save at least 14 percent downtime in operating rooms. For the average hospital, that amounts to millions of dollars and thousands of improved patient outcomes each year.

In essence, this principle underlying genuine business technology is about getting past assumptions and averages to achieve a much clearer picture of the customer based on higher-level science. It is about empowering systems that are capable of adapting, by using data and outcomes, so that they can learn by doing and offer feedback directly into the business intent of an enterprise and recommend changes in real time.

These three principles are the basis for staying alive today and living to see another day with Gen D.

From Dream to Reality

Democratize how you do technology. Use the language of business, not the language of programming, and let business people speak directly. Use technology that can generate code on its own, based on that business language. Think in layers. Marry data and intent in processes that are for the customer, so the customer experience is seamless and corresponds to what Gen D expects and demands. Harness the power of analytics to support what you're doing for customers. Make sure those systems are built to change, not to become dinosaurs that compel business people to go rogue. Support collaboration. Support reuse.

These are the steps to genuine business technology. They address some of the reasons that in a growing number of enterprises, the marketing function is eclipsing the IT function in technology spending. And they go even further.

George Colony, the CEO of Forrester Research, has been touting a shift from information technology to business technology and from technologist to business person for quite some time. "It is taking longer than expected," reported *CIO* magazine back in 2009.

Still, Colony has surely been on to something.

"Changing the term to BT," he told *CIO* magazine back then, "is also a powerful way for the chief technologist—CIO or CTO—to signal to line-of-business managers and executives and also to the presidents, COO, CEO, and the board of directors that 'We're not in the technology business anymore; we're in the real business—the company's business.' I believe by changing the name to BT, and changing its behavior to focus on the business of the business, the technology organization would transform its relationship with the business. I think it would begin to communicate in a different language (the language of business), the current lack of communication would dissipate, and we'd have a higher level of communication around the business problems and the business issues. Which, of course, the presidents and line execs think and care about every day, but all too often, the technologists don't. Changing the name from IT to BT is a way to change the mindset in IT and change the relationship between technologies and business people. Definitely."[41]

Colony is correct, but without the ...
here, the dream of achieving true b·
Without capturing the underlyir
the business works or shoul' _ during them in the language of
the business people them· ...tems will continue to fail the business people who use them.

Without the layer .hat achieves multi-dimensionality, that gives people systems that · κ both up and down and sideways, systems will fail business people ..d never become business technology. Absent the capturing the comr /nalities across silos and channels, and having processes that merge .stomer data with customer and business intent, the unified and enhan :d customer experience that business people absolutely must be prepar d to provide to Gen D will remain a dream.

And witho· .n automation capability by and for business people, the Business Technology objective will remain an elusive one. Anything and everything that can be automated for greater effect should be automated, and the automation has to be so simple and straightforward that no specially trained translator of human language into computer code is needed to do the job. Quite simply, it isn't rocket science, and it doesn't necessarily require the work of IT people to bring it to fruition.

What makes all this possible is the overall model for business technology going forward. It's about ending the reign of two-dimensional systems that don't serve the interest of achieving 1080 customer high-definition. It's about blueprints that can build themselves. It's about technology that actually makes it possible to end the relationship between business and IT based on master craftsman. No more will you need to get an "expert" to design for you, and then hire a craftsman to create an example of what you want, and then contract with manufacturers to create the finished product. Those days— and those kinds of IT roles— can and will come to an end and evolve into higher value roles tied more closely to the business.

Something else will come to an end, too: A certain *insanity* that permeates the software industry. In just about every industry except for software, there's an understanding of the need to go from concept to execution. That understanding got us to computer-aided design (CAD). In so many fields today, computer systems are used to help create, modify, analyze, or optimize designs. Architects design buildings using CAD.

[41] Thomas Wailgum, "You Say IT, Forrester Says BT: What's the Difference" CIO, September 24, 2009, at http://www.cio.com/article/503221/You_Say_IT_Forrester_Says_BT_What_s_the_Difference